ISBN: 9781313446907

Published by:
HardPress Publishing
8345 NW 66TH ST #2561
MIAMI FL 33166-2626

Email: info@hardpress.net
Web: http://www.hardpress.net

DELAWARE CORPORATIONS

A DIGEST OF THE

DECISIONS

AND THE LAW

SECOND EDITION

PRESENTED BY

United States
Corporation Company

Dover, Del.—311 South State Street

Chicago—30 North La Salle Street   Albany, N.Y.— 93 State Street
St. Louis—604 Carleton Building   Jersey City, N.J.—15 Exchange Place
Trenton, N. J.—114 West State Street
Philadelphia—Commonwealth Trust Bldg.
Pittsburgh, Pa.—308 Magee Bldg.

Executive Offices—65 Cedar Street, New York City

B 114 62,

Reasons for Incorporating in Delaware

No requirements as to residence of incorporators or directors.

A broad charter may be obtained with no unnecessary formalities.

Organization meetings may be held without the State.

Capitalization may be any amount not less than $2,000.

Non par value shares may be created, without indicating a stated capital.

No State stamp tax on stock.

Judgment of directors upon issuance of stock is conclusive in the absence of fraud.

Stockholders and directors meetings may be held without the State.

No complicated State reports or financial statements required.

Organization fees and annual taxes are less than in other states.

No State Income Tax on corporations. Non-residents are not taxed on their holdings of stock in Delaware corporations.

ORGANIZATION FEE

The organization fee is ten cents per thousand up to $2,000,000; thereafter at five cents per thousand. Minimum fee is $10. (For taxation purposes only, non par value shares are figured at $100 each). In addition there are incidental filing, certifying and recording charges of about $15.

ANNUAL FRANCHISE TAX

The annual franchise tax is based upon the authorized capital, as follows: $25,000 or under $5. $100,000 or under $10. $300,000 or under $20. $500,000 or under $25. $1,000,000 or under $50; thereafter at the rate of $25 per million. Dormant corporations pay one-half the tax, but not less than $5.

INTRODUCTORY

This Digest has been prepared with the compliments of The UNITED STATES CORPORATION COMPANY, by J. B. R. Smith, Esq., Associate Editor of the Corporation Manual, for distribution among those lawyers who are interested in corporate organizations under the laws of Delaware.

It is divided into two parts. Part One is a comprehensive abstract of the "General Corporation Law" of 1899 with its amendments, to 1920, copiously annotated.

Part Two is a digest of all the cases relating to corporations, of the Delaware courts reported to July 17, 1919.

Both Parts One and Two have the same subject arrangement by the use of which speedy reference to any given subject may be had, both to the Statutes and to the decisions. Both parts have been liberally cross-referenced.

In preparing the digest of decisions, the editor is greatly indebted to the West Publishing Company who very kindly put the invaluable syllabi of the decisions contained in the Atlantic Reporter Digest at his disposal.

In addition to the digest there will be found a compilation of the advantages of the State of Delaware as a domicile for business corporations; also the complete text of the Shares Without Par Value sections of the Corporation Act, together with a brief recital of its special advantages.

3

ADVANTAGES AND BENEFITS OF THE LAW

The advantages and benefits of the general corporation law of the State of Delaware are briefly as follows:—

The law is orderly and simple in arrangement, and, being a complete revision, may be studied and treated as a whole.

There have been few amendments except those intended to simplify the act and the procedure for the operation of Delaware corporations.

The law has stood the test of twenty-one years' examination by counsel and the courts, and there is no disposition to effect changes on the part of the legislature or the people of Delaware.

The law is ably administered by the state officials.

A very broad charter may be secured, granting any number or combination of purposes, excepting insurance and banking, with great flexibility as to provisions of restriction or regulation of the affairs of the corporation.

There are no limitations on the powers of a Delaware corporation with respect to the holding of shares of other corporations or the holding of real and personal property, either within or without the state; provided the charter contains authority for the transaction of business outside of Delaware.

The organization tax is moderate.

The annual tax is low, being fixed in advance upon the authorized capital and is not based upon income.

There is no corporation income tax in Delaware.

The constitution of the state prohibits taxation upon shares of stock held by non-residents; hence there is no state inheritance tax upon non-resident holders of shares.

There is no limitation upon the amount of capital stock nor upon indebtedness; except that the capital stock must be at least two thousand dollars, or at least ten shares in the case of non par value share corporations.

There is no limitation or restriction on the proportion of preferred stocks, neither upon dividends nor upon the par value of shares which may be created.

Shares of stock without any nominal or par value, may be created, and it is not necessary to fix any amount of capital with which the corporation will carry on business.

There is no limitation upon the amount of bonds which may be issued. There is no state tax upon them and by so providing in the certificate of incorporation such bonds may be given voting power.

Par value stock may be issued for labor done, money paid, personal and real property, or leases thereof, and fraud being absent, the judgment of the directors respecting the consideration therefor is conclusive, such stock becoming fully paid and subject to no further call or assessment.

Non par value stock may be issued for such consideration as the directors determine, always subject to the constitutional limitation that no shares may be issued except for labor done, money paid, personal and real property or leases thereof.

Stock dividends are expressly authorized by the law.

Incorporators, directors, officers and stockholders may all be non-residents of Delaware.

All meetings of the incorporators, directors and stockholders may be held outside of Delaware.

Directors are not required, by the law, to be stockholders and may be divided into not more than three classes with respect to tenure of office.

The private property of the stockholders is not subject to the payment of corporate debts if proper provision is made in the certificate of incorporation.

But one annual report is required, which does not inquire into the financial affairs of the corporation.

No books or records are required to be kept in Delaware, except the original or a duplicate stock ledger.

Business may begin with a stock subscription of one thousand dollars, or in the case of non par value shares, with a subscription of ten shares. Such shares need not be paid for until payment is called by the Board of Directors. No amount of cash is required to be paid in.

Voting power may be withheld from any class of stock or voting rights may be restricted in any other manner.

Cumulative voting may be provided for.

The corporation may be completely organized within twenty-four hours by any of our offices.

SHARES WITHOUT PAR VALUE

The Delaware shares without par value act deserves especial consideration. In brevity, flexibility and comprehensiveness it has not been surpassed.

This law regards such "shares" as separate and distinct from "corporate capital," providing that they may be issued for "such consideration" as the directors, pursuant to authority, may provide, subject to the state constitutional provision that "no corporation shall issue stock, except for money paid, labor done or personal property, real estate or leases thereof actually acquired." No minimum or other fixed amount of capital is required with which to begin business nor need the amount of capital at any time be disclosed, though the charter may provide for such disclosure as one of its regulatory provisions if so desired.

Accordingly the corporation may use such shares for the purpose of providing capital, either through direct exchange therefor, or indirectly upon a nominal cash or other constitutional consideration, as an inducement for the sale of preferred stock or of bonds; or upon similar consideration they may be used simply as a basis for vesting the management, or for the distribution of profits or of assets or for all these purposes. This provision, together with the sister one that "different classes" with stated "voting powers or restriction or qualification thereof," may be provided makes convenient the attainment of a variety of results heretofore impossible.

Mutual associations with share capital, heretofore difficult if not impossible, are readily organized, a conspicuous example being the "Copper Export Association" and other mutual export associations recently organized under the Webb Act. Indeed, it may be questioned how such organizations as the Webb Act contemplates may successfully function except through the provisions of legislation similar to the Delaware Act.

Organizations providing "sharing of profits" with employees or others, for distributing or rearranging the voting power and management, in fact for making almost any business arrangement or rearrangement that interest or economy suggests and which may be included in a lawful personal contract, may be formed under this Act.

In all cases where either some peculiar form of organization is desired or intangible assets or prospects of any kind are to be employed the advantages of this law should be considered.

The Law, which is Section 4a and a part of Section 5 of the General Corporation Law, follows in full:

"Sec. 4a. STOCK WITHOUT PAR VALUE:—Any corporation may, if so provided in its Certificate of Incorporation or in an amendment thereof, issue shares of stock (other than stock preferred as to dividends or preferred as to its distributive share of the assets of the corporation or subject to redemption at a fixed price) without any nominal or par value. Every share of such stock without nominal or par value shall be equal to every other share of such stock, except that the Certificate of Incorporation may provide that such stock shall be divided into different classes with such designations and voting powers or restriction or qualification thereof as shall be stated therein, but all such stock shall be subordinate to the preferences given to preferred stock, if any. Such stock may be issued by the corporation from time to time for such consideration as may be fixed from time to time by the Board of Directors thereof, pursuant to authority conferred in the certificate of incorporation, or if such certificate shall not so provide, then by the consent of the holders of two-thirds of each class of stock then outstanding and entitled to vote given at a meeting called for that purpose in such manner as shall be prescribed by the by-laws, and any and all such shares so issued, the full consideration for which has been paid or delivered, shall be deemed full paid stock and not liable to any further call or assessment thereon, and the holder of such shares shall not be liable for any further payments under the provisions of this Chapter.

In any case in which the law requires that the par value of the shares of stock of a corporation be stated in any certificate or paper

7

it shall be stated, in respect of such shares, that such shares are without par value, and wherever the amount of stock, authorized or issued, is required to be stated, the number of shares authorized or issued shall be stated, and it shall also be stated that such shares are without par value. For the purpose of the taxes prescribed to be paid on the filing of any certificate or other paper relating to corporations and of franchise taxes prescribed to be paid by corporations to this State, but for no other purpose, such shares shall be taken to be of the par value of One Hundred Dollars each."

Sec. 5. The Certificate of Incorporation shall set forth:

"* * * * * * * Par. 4. * * * * * in the case of a corporation without nominal or par value to its stock or any class thereof, the certificate of incorporation, with respect to such stock, in lieu of the above shall state the total number of shares authorized and that they are without nominal or par value, and the number of shares with which it will commence business, which shall not be less than ten shares; * * * * * * *"

SUBJECT ARRANGEMENT

I. CORPORATE AUTHORIZATION

1. The constitution.
2. The statutes.

II. CORPORATE PROCEDURE

3. Corporate charters and organization of corporations.
4. Amendment of corporate charters.
5. Merger and consolidation of corporations.
6. Corporate elections and meetings generally.
7. Corporate management and corporation business.
8. Corporation books, notices and records.
9. Corporation reports.
10. Courts, court procedure, pleading and evidence.

III. CORPORATE STRUCTURE

11. Name and seal.
12. Legal domicile and place of business.
13. By-laws.
14. Stock, capital, capital stock.
15. Dividends.

IV. CORPORATE PERSONNEL

16. Incorporators.
17. Stockholders.
18. Voting trusts, trustees and proxies.
19. Directors.
20. Officers.
21. Agents.
22. Employees.

V. CORPORATE POWERS, RIGHTS, DUTIES AND LIMITATIONS

VI. CORPORATE TERMINATION

VII. CORPORATE REORGANIZATION AND EXTENSION

VIII. FEES AND TAXES

IX. FOREIGN CORPORATIONS

PART ONE

The citations in Part I. unless otherwise indicated have reference to the "General Corporation Laws of Delaware." Where "No." followed by number is used, reference is had to that particular number under this "subject arrangement."

I. CORPORATE AUTHORIZATION

1. THE CONSTITUTION

1a. Corporations Shall Not Be Created by special act, nor shall any existing charter be amended, renewed or revived except by general law. These provisions are not applicable to municipal corporations, banks or corporations for charitable, penal, reformatory or educational purposes sustained in whole or in part by the state. (Const. Art. 9, Sec. 1)

2. THE STATUTES

2a. Corporations May Be Established by three or more persons for the transaction of any lawful business under the provisions of an act passed in 1899, amended by the Revised Statutes of 1915 and further amended by the subsequent sessions of the legislature. (Sec. 1.)

NOTE: This provision enables corporations to organize under the General Corporation Law for any lawful purpose or any combination of purposes except those prohibited in the constitution. (See No. 2a above). Accordingly public utility and insurance companies as well as railroad corporations to operate out of the state, may avail themselves of its provisions. Railroad corporations operating within the state are, however, subject to special provisions of the act not included in this digest, and insurance companies, before they can do business within the state must comply with legislation providing for their qualification and operation, and become subject to the jurisdiction of the insurance commissioner.

II. CORPORATE PROCEDURE

3. CORPORATE CHARTERS AND ORGANIZATION OF CORPORATIONS

3a. **The Certificate of Incorporation** which shall set forth:—

(1) NAME, which name shall contain one of the words "association," "company," "corporation," "club," "incorporated," "society," "union," or "syndicate," or one of the abbreviations "co." or "inc." and shall be such as to distinguish it from any other corporation engaged in the same business.

(2) LOCATION OF PRINCIPAL OFFICE IN THIS STATE, and NAME of RESIDENT AGENT, which agent may be either an individual or a corporation.

NOTE: The UNITED STATES CORPORATION COMPANY, whose address is No. 311 South State Street, Dover, Delaware, acts as resident agent and furnishes principal office.

(3) THE NATURE OF THE BUSINESS.

NOTE: A company may provide for any number or any combination of businesses, objects or purposes, including railroads without the state, pipe line corporations, transportation and shipping corporations, corporations for financing purchases, and for any and all usual holding, mercantile and business purposes. For instance: a Delaware corporation may combine a mercantile business with the ownership and operation of ships and may be licensed to do business in New York, whereas the same business under New York statutes would require two domestic corporations.

(4) THE AMOUNT OF THE TOTAL AUTHORIZED CAPITAL STOCK of the corporation, which shall not be less than $2,000. THE NUMBER OF SHARES into which the same is divided and the par value of each share.

NOTE: The par value of the share is not limited.

THE AMOUNT OF CAPITAL STOCK with which it will commence business, which shall not be less than $1,000.

NOTE: This provision refers to "capital stock" and not to the payment of capital, there being no statutory period for the payment of any portion of the capital.

IF WITHOUT PAR VALUE the certificate of incorporation shall state, in lieu of the above, the total number of shares authorized, that they are without par value, (and which under the State Department has ruled, shall be not less than twenty) and the number of shares, not fewer than ten, with which it will commence business.

WHERE SHARES SHALL BE ISSUED BOTH WITH PAR AND WITHOUT PAR, the number of shares of each, together with the class and the par value of those which are to be so issued.

NOTE: The law does not require any amount of stated capital to be set out when non-par value shares are created.

IF MORE THAN ONE CLASS OF STOCK is created there shall be a description of the respective classes with the terms on which they are created.

NOTE: The Delaware law is very flexible with respect to the classes and designations of preferred and other stocks. Formerly the statute required that the amount of outstanding preferred stocks should not exceed two-thirds of the entire amount issued for cash or property, but this provision has been repealed and there is now no statutory limitation. Varying voting rights may be given, or withheld entirely, or may be withheld during a period of non-payment of dividends or in other contingencies.

(5) THE NAMES AND PLACES OF RESIDENCE of each of the original subscribers to the capital stock.

(6) PERIOD OF EXISTENCE, which may be perpetual.

(7) WHETHER THE PRIVATE PROPERTY of the stockholders shall be subject to the payment of corporate debts, and if so, to what extent.

NOTE: It is customary to include under this head in the charter a statement somewhat as follows: "The private property of the stockholders shall not be subject to the payment of corporate debts to any extent whatever."

(8) THE CERTIFICATE OF INCORPORATION MAY ALSO CONTAIN any provision which the incorporators may choose to insert for the regulation of the business or defining the powers of the corporation, of the directors and the stockholders, or of any class of the stockholders; provided such provisions are not contrary to the laws of this state. (Sec. 5)

NOTE: The certificate of incorporation should contain a statement reserving the power to conduct business in other states, the District of Columbia, territories, colonies and foreign countries, and to have offices outside of Delaware and to hold, purchase, mortgage, and convey real and personal property outside of Delaware, if such powers are desired.

3b. **Execution of Certificate of Incorporation** shall be by each of the original subscribers to capital stock signing and sealing the certificate. (Sec. 6).

3c. **Acknowledgment and Execution of Certificate** may be taken within the state before the chancellor, any state or Federal judge, or notary public, or two justices of the peace for the same county; without the state, before any Consul-general, consul, vice-consul, consular agent or commercial agent of the United States, judge of any district or circuit court of the United States, chancellor or any judge of a court of record of any state, territory or country, mayor or chief officer of any city or borough, notary public, or commissioner of deeds appointed by governor. (See Del. Rev. Code S.3205-3209).

NOTE: When certificate is executed in the State of New York, the acknowledgment should be taken before a notary public, the signature of a New York Commissioner of Deeds not being sufficient. The notary must affix his seal of office. No certificate of the County Clerk is required.

3d. **Filing of Certificate** shall be in the office of the Secretary of State who shall furnish a certified copy which shall be:—

3e. **Recorded** in the office of the recorder of the County where the principal office is located. (Sec. 6).

NOTE: When The UNITED STATES CORPORATION COMPANY is named as agent in Delaware, it attends to the filing and recording of the certificate of incorporation and the securing of the necessary certified copies.

3f. **Corporate Existence Begins** upon the filing and recording of the certificate of incorporation and the payment of the license tax. (Sec. 7).

3g. **Provision for Votes By Bondholders** may be made in the original or amended certificate of incorporation, and such other power as stockholders have may likewise be conferred on such bondholders. (Sec. 29).

NOTE: Attention of Counsel is called to the fact that a corporation by providing a comparatively small capital stock and a large bond issue may materially reduce the organization fees and annual taxes by giving voting power and other rights of stockholders to the bondholders.

4. AMENDMENT OF CORPORATE CHARTERS

4a. **Amendment Before Payment of Capital** may be made by executing, filing and recording an amended certificate signed by the original incorporators in the manner required for original certificates. (Sec. 25).

NOTE: In practice, amendment before "payment of capital" is also taken to mean before the commencement of the business of the corporation. It would be unusual for the incorporators to amend the charter after business had been commenced or directors elected, even though no part of the capital might have been paid in.

4b. **Amendment to Certificate of Incorporation After Payment** of any part of capital may be made for the purpose of adding to or limiting corporate powers, substituting other powers, increasing or decreasing its authorized capital stock, changing the number and par value of its shares, changing its corporate title or making any other change in its charter, provided that such amendment shall contain only such provisions as would be lawful to insert in an original certificate. (Sec. 26).

4c. **An Amendment Is Made** by a resolution of the board of directors declaring its advisability, and calling a stockholders' meeting, at which, if a majority of the entire stock entitled to vote, or if the amendment changes the preferences, a majority of each class of stock affected, regardless of voting rights, favor the amendment, a certificate thereof is filed with the Secretary of State and recorded with the recorder of the proper county and the amendment thereupon becomes effective. (Sec. 26).

NOTE: Detailed procedure for making an amendment of the certificate of incorporation is found in section 26 of the General Corporation Law. If a reduction in the capital stock is contemplated the provisions of section 28 must also be considered.

5. MERGER AND CONSOLIDATION OF CORPORATIONS

5a. **Power to Merge.** Any two or more Delaware Corporations may consolidate into a single corporation which may be either one of said consolidated corporations or a new corporation. (Sec. 59).

NOTE: The procedure and the powers of merged corporations are set out at length in sections 59 to 64 inclusive of the General Corporation Law.

6. CORPORATE ELECTIONS AND MEETINGS

6a. **Every Stockholder** shall be entitled to one vote in person or by proxy for each share of capital stock unless otherwise provided in the certificate of incorporation or amendment thereto. (Sec. 17).

For determination of stockholders entitled to vote see No. 10a below (Sec. 29).

NOTE: It is possible to provide in the certificate of incorporation different voting powers for different classes of stock, to withhold

15

the vote absolutely from any class or classes, to provide that certain classes shall vote only during a period when dividends are not paid, or for any other contingency of a similar nature. It is also possible to provide that holders of bonds shall have voting power.

6b. Proxies. See Nos. 18b and 18c.

6c. Shares of Stock Transferred on the books of the corporation within twenty days preceding election of directors shall not be voted upon at such election. (Sec. 17).

6d. Cumulative Voting may be provided for in the certificate of incorporation. (Sec. 17).

NOTE: The certificate of incorporation may provide that each stockholder may be entitled to as many votes as shall equal the number of his shares multiplied by the number of directors to be elected and such votes may be cast for a single director or distributed among directors to be elected. In this way a minority interest may be secured in its representation in the board of directors.

6e. Persons Holding Stock in a Fiduciary Capacity shall be entitled to vote the shares so held. (Sec. 18).

6f. Persons Whose Stock Is Pledged shall be entitled to vote such stock unless by the transfer the pledgor shall be expressly empowered on the books of the corporation to vote thereon. (Sec. 18).

6g. Shares of Its Own Capital Stock belonging to the corporation shall not be voted upon, either directly or indirectly. (Sec. 19).

6h. An Alphabetical List of Stockholders shall be open for ten days at the place of election for the examination of any stockholder. (Sec. 29).

6i. All Elections of Directors unless otherwise provided in the certificate of incorporation shall be by ballot. (Sec. 30).

6j. The First Meeting for the Election of Directors and the transaction of any other business shall be held at a place either within or without the state fixed by a majority of the incorporators in writing. (Sec. 30).

NOTE: Formerly it was the opinion of some Delaware attorneys that the first meeting of incorporators for the election of directors should be held in Delaware; but the legislature amended section 30 of the corporation law giving specific authority for holding this meeting without the State. The UNITED STATES CORPORATION COMPANY has in its files an opinion of the attorney general of Delaware advising to this effect.

6k. Subsequent Election of Directors shall be at time and place (within or without the State) named in the By-Laws, and such place shall not be changed within sixty days before the election is held. Notice of any change should be given to each stockholder twenty days before the election. (S. 30).

NOTE: Under the authority of section thirty all meetings, either of stockholders, directors or incorporators may be held outside the State of Delaware; but care should be taken to give the statutory notice of change of place of the annual election of directors, if such change is made.

6l. **Stockholders' and Directors' Meetings** may be held at offices outside the state if the By-Laws so provide. (Sec. 30 and 32).

6m. **Vacancies in the Board of Directors** shall be filled by the board unless otherwise provided in the By-Laws. (Sec. 30).

6n. **On Failure to Elect Directors** on the day designated in the By-Laws, the directors shall cause the election to be held as soon thereafter as conveniently may be, or the Chancellor may summarily call the election on the application of any stockholder. (Sec. 31).

6o. **Manner of Voting At Stockholders' Meetings.** Elections of directors, unless the certificate of incorporation otherwise provides, shall be by ballot. (Sec. 30).

NOTE: It is customary also to provide in the By-Laws that any amendment to the By-Laws shall be by ballot and that all other questions may be determined by a viva voce vote of a majority of the stockholders present in person or by proxy, but that any qualified voter may demand a stock vote which must thereupon immediately be taken. All stock votes must be by ballot and all votes by ballot shall state the name of the stockholder voting and the number of shares voted by him, and if by proxy, it shall also state the name of such proxy. Vote upon amendment to certificate of incorporation and mergers must be by ballot at stockholders' meetings.

7. CORPORATE MANAGEMENT AND CORPORATE BUSINESS

7a. **Management Prior to Election of Directors** shall be in the incorporators. (Sec. 8).

7b. **Management After Election of Directors** shall be in the directors who shall hold office until their successors are elected and qualify. (Sec. 9).

NOTE: It is the intent of the statute that directors shall be elected annually unless provision is made for classification.

7c. Quorum of directors shall consist of a majority of board. (Sec. 9).

7d. Executive Committee may be created by the directors having such powers as the By-Laws or the directors shall prescribe. (Sec. 9).

NOTE: This, committee to the extent provided in the resolution of the directors, may exercise the powers of the board of directors in the management of the corporation including the power to authorize the affixing of the corporate seal to any corporate papers.

7e. Directors May Be Arranged in Classes with terms expiring in periods of one, two or three years, if the stockholders or the charter so authorize. (Sec. 9).

7f. First Meeting of Incorporators May Be Held By waiver of notice signed by all of the incorporators or by notice signed by a majority of the incorporators by publication in the county where the corporation has its principal place of business two weeks in advance of the time of meeting, or on two days personal notice to incorporators. (Sec. 11).

7g. By-laws shall be made and altered by the stockholders unless the certificate of incorporation confers that power on the directors; but the stockholders may amend or repeal by-laws made by the directors. (Sec. 12). Also see No. 13 of this pamphlet.

NOTE: It is customary for the incorporators to adopt the By-Laws at their first meeting.

7h. Certificate of Payment of Capital Stock shall be made upon the written request of any creditor or stockholder stating the amount of the installments or calls paid in cash, or by the purchase of property, and the total amount of the capital stock issued, which within thirty days shall be filed with the Secretary of State. (Sec. 23).

7i. Failure for Thirty Days to Comply with said request (No. 7h. above) renders neglecting officers jointly and severally liable for all debts contracted after making such payment and before the filing of such certificate. (Sec. 24).

7j. Stock Ledger shall be open to examination during usual business hours at the principal office to every stockholder. (Sec. 29).

NOTE: The statute provides that this may be an original or a duplicate stock ledger. In practice the keeping of a duplicate stock ledger at the principal office in Delaware is regarded as a complete compliance with the requirement. The UNITED STATES CORPORATION COMPANY as resident agent keeps the duplicate stock ledger and provides each corporation with transfer sheets for reporting issues and transfers of stock, in order that the stock ledger may be kept up to date.

7k. **The Principal Office** or place of business must be maintained within the state with a resident agent in charge thereof. (Sec. 32).

NOTE: The resident agent may be an individual or a corporation. The UNITED STATES CORPORATION COMPANY maintains the principal office in Delaware for many corporations and performs all the duties of resident agent. The appointment of a corporation secures a continuing agency which is not subject to change by reason of death or removal from the locality as in the case of an individual agent.

7l. **The Corporate Name** must be displayed at principal office. (Sec. 33).

NOTE: The UNITED STATES CORPORATION COMPANY displays for each corporation which it represents the corporate name and sign required by statute.

8. CORPORATION BOOKS, NOTICES AND RECORDS

8a. **Corporation Books and Records** may be kept out of the state, but the original or a duplicate stock ledger, at all times during usual business hours shall be open to examination of stockholders at principal office within the state, and a list of stockholders shall be open at least ten days before every election at the place of election for the inspection of those entitled to vote. (Sec. 29).

8b. **Waiver of Notice.** When any notice whatever is required by law or the provisions of the charter or by-laws, a waiver thereof in writing signed by the person entitled to such notice, whether before or after the time stated therein, shall be equivalent to such notice. (Sec. 80).

8c. **Notice of First Meeting.** See No. 7f.

8d. **Notice of Amendment to Charter.** See No. 4.

8e. **Notice of Dissolution.** See No. 30.

8f. **Notice of Sale of Unpaid Stock** shall be by advertisement once a week for three weeks in some newspaper in the county where the corporation is established and mailed to the delinquent stockholder at least twenty days before the sale. (Sec. 22).

9. CORPORATION REPORTS

9a. **Statutory Reports and Annual Reports.** There is but one report required which must be made on or before the first Tuesday in January to the Secretary of State, stating specifically:

(1) LOCATION OF PRINCIPAL OFFICE.

(2) NAME OF AGENT upon whom service of process may be served.

(3) LOCATION OR LOCATIONS of the place or places of business without the State.

(4) NAMES AND ADDRESSES of all the directors and officers of the corporation and when the term of each expires.

(5) THE DATE APPOINTED FOR THE NEXT ANNUAL MEETING.

(6) THE AMOUNT OF AUTHORIZED CAPITAL STOCK and the amount actually issued.

(7) THE AMOUNT INVESTED IN REAL ESTATE.

(8) THE TAX ANNUALLY THEREON and the amount invested in manufacturing or mining, or both, in this state, and if exempt from taxation under the provisions of sections 68, 72 and 83 of this chapter, the specific facts entitling the said corporation to exemption aforesaid. (Sec. 66 Franchise Tax Act). (Sec. No. 35b).

10. COURTS, COURT PROCEDURE, PLEADING AND EVIDENCE

10a. **The Original or Duplicate Stock Ledger** shall be the only evidence of stockholders entitled to examine the list of stockholders prepared for the annual meeting, or to vote thereat, and said original or duplicate stock ledger shall be evidence in all courts in Delaware. (Sec. 29).

10b. **Upon Dissolution** for any cause, the Court of Chancery on the application of a creditor or stockholder may either continue directors as trustees or appoint receivers with general powers and duties of such officers. (Sec. 43).

10c. **Actions Do Not Abate** upon dissolution or expiration of franchise. (Sec. 46).

10d. **Decree of Forfeiture of Charter or of Dissolution** by Court of Chancery shall be filed in the office of the Secretary of State and notice thereof published in the session laws. (Sec. 47).

10e. **Service of Legal Process on Corporations** may be made on the President, or if he resides out of the State, on the Secretary or one of the directors, or upon the resident agent. If after due diligence such officers cannot be served, service may be had on the Secretary of State who shall notify the corporation thereof at its last resident office. (Sec. 48).

NOTE: It is the practice in Delaware to make service upon the resident agent of the corporation; and it is of the utmost importance to each Delaware corporation to have at all times a resident agent in charge of the principal office. By the appointment of the UNITED STATES CORPORATION COMPANY as resident agent the corporation is assured of the proper service of legal documents, as well as the receipt of important mail or other communications.

10f. Actions May Be Had Against Officers, Directors or Stockholders liable for the debts of the corporation, and such officers, directors or stockholders may recover the amount so paid on behalf of the corporation out of the property of the corporation, but not out of the property of any stockholders. No suit shall be brought against any director or stockholder for any corporate debt until execution against the corporation has been returned unsatisfied. (Sec. 49, 50, 51).

10g. Proof of Claims; When Barred. Creditors shall make proof of claims within six months from the date of appointment of receiver or trustee or sooner if the court shall order, and failing to do so upon order of the court may be barred from participation in the distribution of the assets. The court may also prescribe what notice shall be given creditors. (Sec. 53).

10h. Adjudication of Claims. Receiver shall notify all creditors whose claims are disputed, within thirty days after expiration of time for filing thereof, requiring such creditors to submit themselves to such examination as the receiver shall direct; but any creditor may within ten days require the receiver to certify the claim to the Court of Chancery, or he may appeal to that court from the decision of the receiver. (Sec. 54).

10i. Receivers May Sell All Perishable Property free from incumbrance upon order of the court. (Sec. 56).

10j. When Sale of Franchise and Property shall be made, the purchasers may reorganize the corporation with all the rights, privileges and franchises, and subject to all the restrictions of the original corporation. (Sec. 65).

10k. Sale of Franchise and Property under order of court shall be made upon such terms as the court shall decree. (Sec. 66).

10l. Want of Legal Organization shall not be a defense to any action, but this provision shall not be considered to prevent judicial inquiry into the regularity of the organization. (Sec. 68).

10m. No Corporation Shall Plead Usury in any suit to enforce the payment of its bonds or mortgages. (Sec. 78).

10n. Certified Copy of Certificate of Incorporation with Record of Recording shall be evidence in all courts in Delaware. (Sec. 6).

III. CORPORATE STRUCTURE
11. NAME AND SEAL

11a. Corporate Name. See No. 3a (1).

11b. Corporations Using the Word "Trust" in their title shall be under supervision of the Insurance Commissioner and no other corporation shall advertise or put forth any sign as a trust company or in any way transact business as a trust company. (Sec. 83, 84, 85).

11c. Change of Name. See No. 4.

11d. Name Must Be Displayed at principal office; failure to do so subjects corporation to a fine of $100.00. See No. 7. (Sec. 33).

11d. Corporate Seal may be made, altered and used by every corporation. (Sec. 2).

12. LEGAL DOMICILE AND PLACE OF BUSINESS

12a. Principal Office. See No. 7k.

12b. Change of Location of Principal Office Within the State may be made upon resolution adopted at a regular or special meeting of the board and filing and recording certificate thereof as in case of original certificates of incorporation. (Sec. 79).

12c. Offices May Be Maintained Out of the State. See No. 23a. (8).

NOTE: The power conferred in this section enables Delaware corporations, when provision is made therefor in the certificate of incorporation, to engage in interstate business and also to transact intra-state business in all states and countries subject only to the provisions of the various states and countries for the regulation of foreign corporations. The UNITED STATES CORPORATION COMPANY maintains a department for the securing of licenses to do business as foreign corporations in the various states and countries.

13. BY-LAWS

13a. Power to Make by-laws not inconsistent with the constitution or the State laws, including fixing the number of directors, (which may be changed if provision is made therefor), to manage its affairs and to transfer its stock, is given the corporation (No. 23a), to be exercised by the stockholders, or by the directors, if provision is made in the certificate of incorporation. (No. 7g) (Sec. 2 and 12).

13b. Directors May Be Given Power by the By-Laws to fix the amount of the reserve or surplus. (Sec. 34).

13c. **Vacancies in Board** filled as By-Laws prescribe. (Sec. 2, 10, 30).

13d. **Regulation of Elections** provided in By-Laws. (Sec. 30).

13e. **Transfer of Shares** shall be provided for in By-Laws. (Sec. 2).

13f. **The By-Laws Usually Include** among other things provisions for convening and fixing time and place of holding both stockholders' and directors' meetings, including annual, regular, periodical and special meetings, the method of conducting all meetings and the manner of voting thereat, the fixing of quorum, the manner of election of officers and fixing their powers and duties, setting out both the general and the specific powers of the corporation, the filling of vacancies among officers and directors, including authority of directors to increase their number, the mode of transferring shares, the location of the principal office and a requirement to keep duplicate stock ledger at such office, provisions for waiving notices and, finally, the method of amending the By-Laws. (Ed.)

14. STOCK, CAPITAL, CAPITAL STOCK

14a. **Minimum Amount of Authorized Capital** shall be $2,000; of subscribed capital, $1,000; of shares without par value, twenty shares. (Sec. 5).

14b. **Classes of Stock** may be created with such designations, preferences and voting powers, restrictions or qualifications as shall be expressed in certificate of incorporation, (See No. 3) which may be increased or decreased. (See No. 4). (Sec. 13).

NOTE: When preferred stock is authorized with a preference as to dividends, the dividend rate must be fixed.

14c. **Redemption of Preferred Stock** may be provided for at such time and price, not less than par, as may be expressed in the certificate of incorporation. (Sec. 13).

14d. **Issue of Stock for Labor or Property.** Stock subscriptions may be paid for by cash, by labor done or by real or personal property or leases thereof, and the stock so issued shall be fully paid. In the absence of fraud the judgment of the directors as to the value of such labor or property shall be conclusive. (Sec. 14).

NOTE: Such stock issued in accordance with the terms of the resolution of the board of directors is fully paid and non-assessable and is not subject to further call. The power of the directors is absolute on the issuance of stock and to reverse their judgment conclusive fraud must be proven.

STOCK SHALL NOT BE ISSUED except for money paid, labor

done or for personal or real property or leases thereof actually acquired by such corporation. (Const. 9, Sec. 3).

NOTE: In appraising the value of the labor done or of the personal or real property or of the leases of such property, the judgment of the directors is final unless actual fraud is found.

14e. Certificates of Shares. Every stockholder shall have a certificate signed by the President or Vice-President and the Treasurer or the Assistant Treasurer or the Secretary or the Assistant Secretary. (Sec. 15).

14f. Transfer of Shares shall be had on the books of the corporation under such regulations as the by-laws prescribe. If for collateral, the entry shall so state. (Sec. 16).

14g. Stock Is Not Taxable in Delaware when the same shall be owned by persons or corporations without the state. (Const. Art. 9, Sec. 6).

NOTE: This is particularly important to non-resident holders of stock in Delaware corporations, in view of the fact that the constitutional prohibition is held to include a prohibition against the imposition of an inheritance tax.

14h. Capital Must Not Be Impaired By any corporation purchasing its own capital stock. (Sec. 19).

14i. Directors May Accept Subscriptions for Corporate Stock to the amount authorized in the certificate of incorporation and may assess upon each share not fully paid such sum as the business may require, not exceeding the unpaid balance due at par. (Sec. 21).

14j. Failure to Pay Such Assessments may result in an action at law, or unpaid shares may be sold at public sale. (Sec. 22).

14k. Certificate of Payment of Capital Stock. See No. 7.

14l. Increase of Capital Stock. See No. 4.

14m. Reduction of Capital Stock. The *authorized* capital stock may be "decreased" by following the procedure for amending certificates of incorporation (See No. 4) outlined in section twenty-s.\ of the act, adding a recital in the certificate of amendment from section twenty-eight, that all "debts that are not otherwise fully secured have been paid and discharged." Where the *issued* capital stock is to be "reduced" procedure is had under section twenty-eight, requiring a two-thirds stock vote. Accordingly, when both the *authorized* capital stock is to be "decreased" and the *issued* stock is to be "reduced" two certificates of amendment are filed. (Ed.).

14n. Decrease of Capital Stock may be accomplished:—

(1) BY RETIRING OR REDUCING any class of stock.

(2) **BY DRAWING** the necessary number of shares by lot for retirement.

(3) **BY SURRENDER** of every stockholder of his shares and the issue to him in lieu thereof of the decreased number of shares.

(4) **BY THE PURCHASE** at not above par of certain shares for retirement.

(5) **BY RETIRING** shares owned by the corporation

(6) **BY REDUCING** the par value of shares. (Sec. 28).

14o. **Lost Or Destroyed Stock Certificates.** Corporations may issue new certificates of stock in the place of those lost or destroyed and the directors may require the owner to give adequate indemnifying bonds. In case of refusal the owner may apply to the Superior Court of Delaware for an order to show cause and the court shall have jurisdiction to make such order as may appear proper. (Sec. 69, 70).

14p. **Situs of Ownership of Capital Stock.** For all purposes of title, action, attachment, garnishment and court jurisdiction but **not for taxation,** situs of ownership shall be in Delaware. (Sec. 72).

14q. **Stock Without Par Value** may be issued. (Sec. 4a).

NOTE: This is done by appropriate provision in the certificate of incorporation or an amendment thereto. For full text of shares without par value act, see section on that subject immediately preceding Part I of this book.

14r. **Purchase of Corporation's Own Stock.** Every corporation may purchase and sell its own capital stock provided the corporate capital be not impaired thereby. Such stock, however, shall not be voted either directly or indirectly. (Sec. 19).

15. DIVIDENDS

15a. **Preferred Stock Dividends** shall be paid at such rates and on such conditions as shall be stated in the certificate of incorporation, or amendment thereto, which shall be paid before dividends shall be paid on the common stock. (Sec. 13).

NOTE: The rate of dividends must be fixed in the certificate of incorporation. A variable or sliding scale of dividends is not provided for in the statute, nor will a charter be accepted for filing by the Secretary of State containing such provisions.

15b. **Common Stock Dividends** may be paid out of surplus remaining after preferred stock dividends have been provided for. (Sec 13).

15c. **Cumulative Dividends** may be paid on preferred stock if the certificate of incorporation so provides. (Sec. 13).

15d. **Holders of Preferred Stock** are not personally liable in any event for the debts of the corporation, but in case of insolvency all liabilities must be paid in preference to preferred stock. (Sec. 13).

NOTE: By so providing in the certificate of incorporation common stockholders as well as preferred stockholders are relieved from any liability to have their private property subject to the payment of corporate debts. (Sec. 5).

15e. **Dividends May Be Declared** by directors amounting to the whole of the accumulated profits in excess of reserve, which reserve may be determined by the stockholders or by directors if so provided in the by-laws. (Sec. 34).

15f. **Dividends** shall not be paid except from surplus or net profits, and may be in cash or capital stock at par or in case of stock without par value at the price fixed by directors. (Sec. 35).

15g. **Directors Shall Be Liable** jointly and severally for wilfully or negligently paying illegal dividends except those who shall have entered their dissent on the minutes, or by publishing such dissent. (Sec. 35).

IV. CORPORATE PERSONNEL

16. INCORPORATORS

16a. **At Least Three Incorporators** are necessary who must sign the certificate of incorporation. (Sec. 1, 5).

NOTE: Incorporators may be either residents or non-residents of Delaware, the only qualification stated in the law being that they shall be persons and not fewer than three in number.

16b. **Management Prior to Election of Directors** shall be in the incorporators. (Sec. 7).

16c. **Incorporators Hold First Meeting.** See No. 7 above. (Sec. 11).

NOTE: This meeting may be held either in Delaware or outside the State, and notice may be waived. It is customary at this meeting to elect the directors and to adopt the by-laws.

17. STOCKHOLDERS

17a. **Stockholders' Liability** for debts if any shall be stated in the certificate of incorporation. (Sec. 5).

NOTE: By referring to 3a, sub-division seven, and to 15d of this pamphlet, it will be seen that by so providing in the certificate of incorporation the private property of stockholders is relieved from all liability for corporate debts.

17b. **Stockholder's Liability** enforced. See No. 14j.

17c. **The Original or Duplicate Stock Ledger.** See No. 7j.

17d. The Amount of Surplus or Reserve shall be determined by the stockholders except when this power is conferred by the certificate of incorporation on the directors. (Sec. 34).

18. VOTING TRUSTS, TRUSTEES AND PROXIES

18a.–Voting Trustees. No statutory provision.

NOTE: Voting trusts, however, have been in common use for years in Delaware and have never been voided in any court proceeding, so far as can be determined.

18b. Proxies may be voted on for not longer than three years unless they provide for a longer period. (Sec. 17).

18c. Stockholders May Vote by proxy. (Sec. 17).

19. DIRECTORS

19a. Qualification of Directors. Directors shall be at least three in number and unless classified, which classification may be for one, two or three years, they shall be elected annually and serve until their successors qualify. (Sec. 9).

NOTE: Formerly each director was required to hold at least three shares of stock in the corporation and at least one director was required to be a resident of Delaware. In 1915 an amendment to the law repealed the requirement for a resident director and in 1917 another amendment repealed the requirement that directors must be shareholders; therefore directors no longer need be stockholders of the corporation, it not being necessary at common law that the director be a stockholder. (See Cook on Corporations, eighth edition, volume three, section 623, and Fletcher's Encyclopedia of Corporations, volume three, section 1771, and cases cited.)

19b. Directors neglecting or refusing to produce the required alphabetical list of stockholders at any election shall be ineligible to any office at such election. (Sec. 29).

19c. Directors Shall Be Liable for any loss or damage resulting from the publication of any written statement or report of the condition of the business known by them to be false in any material respect. (Sec. 37).

19d. Directors Shall Be Liable for debts in default of publication of decrease of capital stock. (Sec. 28).

19e. No Loan of Any Money shall be made to any officer. (Sec. 36).

19f. General Powers of Directors. The board of directors shall have the management of the business of the company and, subject to the restrictions imposed by law, by the certificate of incorporation or by the By-Laws, may exercise all the powers of the corporation. (Ed.)

19g. Specific Powers of Directors. It is usual to include in the By-Laws certain specific powers which may be exercised without prejudice to the general powers and which may include:

(1) THE SELECTION of the common seal.

(2) TO MAKE REGULATIONS NOT INCONSISTENT WITH THE BY-LAWS for the management of its affairs.

(3) TO PURCHASE AND PAY for the corporate property, rights and privileges.

(4) TO BORROW MONEY and to make and issue notes, bonds and other evidences of debt secured or unsecured by corporate mortgages.

(5) TO APPOINT the necessary subordinate officers and agents and to fix their duties, tenure and salaries, removing such officers for cause.

(6) TO DETERMINE who shall be authorized to make and sign bills, notes, checks, receipts, contracts, etc.

(7) TO DETERMINE who shall be entitled to vote in the name of the company and to assign and transfer stock, bonds or other securities of other corporations held by the company.

(8) TO DELEGATE any of the ordinary business powers of the board to standing or special committees, officers or agents, with power to sub-delegate. (Ed.)

20. OFFICERS

20a. How Elected, Duty, Tenure, Vacancies. Every corporation shall have a President, Secretary and Treasurer chosen by the directors or stockholders who shall hold their offices until their successors qualify. (Sec. 10).

NOTE: It is customary for the By-Laws to provide that officers shall be chosen by the directors.

20b. Qualification of Officers. The President shall be a director. The Secretary shall be sworn to the faithful discharge of his duties. The Secretary and Treasurer may be the same person. The Vice-President, if any, may also hold the office of Vice-President and Treasurer or Vice-President and Secretary, but not both. The Treasurer may be required to give bond as the by-laws shall provide. (Sec. 10).

20c. Duties of Officers. It is customary for the By-Laws to prescribe the specific duties of the officers which are substantially as follows:—

(1) PRESIDENT: The President shall preside at all directors' meetings and shall be the chairman at stockholders' meetings. He

shall have power to appoint and discharge, subject to directors' approval, employees, and to fix their compensation; to make contracts and agreements in the name of the company and, while the directors or the executive committee are not in session, he shall have general management of the corporate business. He shall generally do all acts incident to the office of President or which are otherwise authorized or required by law.

(2) VICE-PRESIDENT: The Vice-President shall perform the duties of the President in the President's absence and shall have such other powers as shall be prescribed by the directors.

(3) SECRETARY: The Secretary shall give notice of all stockholders' and directors' meetings and shall likewise give all other legal notices and upon refusal to do so, such notice may be given by any person directed by the President. The Secretary shall record all the proceedings of the corporation and of the directors and shall perform such other duties as may be assigned him by the directors. He shall have custody of the corporate seal and shall be sworn to the faithful discharge of his duties.

(4) TREASURER: The Treasurer shall have the custody of the funds, securities and valuable documents of the company. He shall give receipts and shall pay out of the funds on hand all just debts. He shall keep accurate accounts of all moneys received and paid out, and whenever required by the President or directors shall render a statement thereof keeping all such books as are necessary to record the financial transactions of the company, including the stock and transfer books; and he is usually the officer designated to have supervision over the stock and securities of the company. He shall give bond for the faithful discharge of his duties. (Ed.)

NOTE: The UNITED STATES CORPORATION COMPANY will furnish to counsel approved By-Laws containing these provisions.

20d. **Other Officers.** Corporations may have such other officers, agents and factors as may be deemed necessary, who may be chosen as provided in the By-Laws or as determined by directors with such qualifications and bonds as may be prescribed. (Sec. 10).

20e. **Vacancies.** May be filled in the manner prescribed in the By-Laws or, in the absence of such provision, by the directors. (Sec. 10).

20f. **The Officer in Charge of the Stock Ledger** shall make a list, ten days prior to the election of directors, of stockholders entitled to vote, arranged in alphabetical order. (Sec. 29).

NOTE: This list is required to be open to the examination of any stockholder at the place where the election is to be held, for ten days previous to the election, and must also Le produced at the annual meeting for the inspection of any stockholder present.

20g. Officers Making Loan Shall Be Liable for any loan of money to an officer, or to a stockholder upon the security of the stock of the corporation. (Sec. 36).

NOTE: The statute specifically prohibits such loans. (Sec. 36).

21. AGENTS

21a. Resident Agent must be in charge of principal office in the state. (Sec. 32).

NOTE: The duty of the resident agent in addition to the responsibility of being in charge of the registered office is to keep the name of the corporation displayed, to maintain the original or duplicate stock ledger and to receive process papers, notices, etc. when served. The UNITED STATES CORPORATION COMPANY maintains the principal office in the state of Delaware and performs all of these duties with accuracy, promptness and dispatch. The company as agent also notifies the Delaware corporation when to hold its annual meeting, when annual reports must be filed and furnishes blanks therefor, secures tax bills and attends to their payment; and also gives to counsel the benefit at all times of its experience.

21b. Necessary Agents may be appointed and compensated as provided in the By-Laws. (Sec. 2, 10).

22. EMPLOYEES

22a. Lien for Wages of Employees of Insolvent Corporations shall be paid before any other debt but shall not extend for a longer period than two months, and the word "employee" shall not include the officers of the corporation. (Sec. 57).

V. CORPORATE POWERS, RIGHTS, DUTIES AND LIMITATIONS

23. CORPORATE POWERS

23a. General Powers. Every corporation created under the provisions of this chapter shall have power:—

(1) TO HAVE SUCCESSION, by its corporate name, for the time stated in its certificate of incorporation, and when no period is limited, it shall be perpetual.

(2) TO SUE AND TO BE SUED, complain and defend in any court of law or equity.

(3) TO MAKE AND USE a common seal, and alter the same at pleasure.

(4) TO HOLD, PURCHASE AND CONVEY REAL AND PERSONAL ESTATE, and to mortgage and lease any such real and personal estate with its franchises; the power to hold real and personal estate, except in the case of religious corporations, shall include the power to take the same by devise or bequest.

(5) TO APPOINT SUCH OFFICERS AND AGENTS as the business of the corporation shall require and to allow them suitable compensation.

(6) TO MAKE BY-LAWS not inconsistent with the Constitution or laws of the United States or of this State, fixing and altering the number of its directors, for the management of its property, the regulation and government of its affairs and for the certification and transfer of its stock, with penalties for the breach thereof not exceeding twenty dollars.

(7) TO WIND UP AND DISSOLVE ITSELF, or to be wound up and dissolved in the manner hereinafter mentioned.

(8) TO CONDUCT BUSINESS in this State, other States, the District of Columbia, the territories and colonies of the United States and in foreign countries, and have one or more offices out of this State, and to hold, purchase, mortgage and convey real and personal property out of this State, provided such powers are included within the objects set forth in its certificate of incorporation. (Sec. 2).

23b. **Additional Powers** shall include:

(1) ALL THE POWERS AND PRIVILEGES contained in the General Corporation Law.　(Sec. 3).

(2) THE POWERS expressly given in the Certificate of Incorporation. (Sec. 3).

NOTE: The corporation may also insert in its certificate of incorporation, provisions for the regulation of the business and for defining the powers of the corporation, directors and stockholders, and may secure additional rights and powers not expressly given by statute, provided such rights and powers do not contravene the laws of Delaware.

23c. **Sale, Lease or Exchange of Entire Assets and Franchises** may be made by the directors at any meeting when authorized by a majority of the outstanding stock having voting power given at a meeting duly called for that purpose or when authorized by the written consent of the majority of holders of such stock. (Sec. 64a).

23d. **Corporations May Guarantee, Purchase, Hold, Sell, Assign, Transfer, Mortgage, Pledge or Otherwise Dispose of** shares of the capital stock, or any bonds, securities or evidences of indebtedness created by any other corporation, and while owner of said stock may exercise all the privileges of ownership including the right to vote thereon. (Sec. 77).

24. CORPORATE RIGHTS

24a. **Statutory Corporate Rights** are as set out in the Constitution and Statutes and herewith digested.

24b. **Legal Corporate Rights** thus far considered by the court are as found digested in Part 2 No. 24.

25. CORPORATE DUTIES

25a. **Statutory Corporate Duties** are likewise as set out in the Constitution and Statutes and herewith digested.

25b. **Legal Corporate Duties** thus far considered by the courts accordingly will be found in Part 2 No. 25.

26. CORPORATE DISABILITIES AND LIMITATIONS

26a. **Restrictions, Liabilities and Powers.** Said corporations shall be subject to the restrictions and liabilities of the general corporation law and shall not possess or exercise any other powers except such as are incidental to those herein conferred. (Sec. 3).

26b. **Corporations Shall Not Make Loan of Money** to any officer nor to any stockholder upon the security of the stock of the corporation, nor shall any corporation take as security for any debt, a lien on any part of its capital stock, except to prevent loss from a debt previously contracted. (Sec. 36).

NOTE: Any officer assenting to loan to an officer of the corporation, or to a stockholder upon security of the stock of the corporation, shall be liable to the corporation until payment of the loan with interest.

VI. CORPORATE TERMINATION

27. PERIOD OF EXISTENCE

27a. **Corporate Existence Begins** upon filing and recording of certificate of incorporation. (Sec. 7).

27b. **Corporate Existence Continues** for a term of years or perpetually as set out in the charter. (Sec. 5).

27c. **Corporate Existence After Expiration of Franchise or Dissolution** for any cause, continues for three years for purpose of suit and liquidation but not for continuing business. (Sec. 40).

28. TERMINATION OF CORPORATE FRANCHISE

28a. **Forfeiture of Certificate of Incorporation.** The legislature shall by General Law provide for the forfeiture of certificate of incorporation of all corporations for abuse, misuse or non-use. (Const. 9, Sec. 1).

29. FORFEITURE OF CORPORATE FRANCHISE AND REVOCATION OF CHARTER

29a. Failure to Elect Directors at designated time shall not work forfeiture. (Sec. 31).

29b. Jurisdiction to Revoke Certificates of Incorporation for abuse, misuse or non-use is in the Court of Chancery. The attorney general on his own motion or on relation of proper parties shall represent the State, and the Court of Chancery shall have power to appoint receivers or otherwise to administer or wind up the affairs of the corporation whose charter shall be thus revoked or forfeited. (Sec. 67).

NOTE: Such revocation, however, cannot be made until at least two years after the filing of the certificate of incorporation.

29c. Revocation of Charter for Non-Payment of Taxes shall be made after two consecutive years neglect or refusal to pay to the state any tax or taxes assessed against the corporation. (Sec. 74 of the Franchise Tax Act).

NOTE: There are provisions, however, for reinstatement of the corporation upon payment of the back taxes. See section 81 of the Franchise Tax Law.

30. VOLUNTARY DISSOLUTION

30a. Surrender of Corporate Rights Before Payment of Capital Stock may be made by filing with the Secretary of State a verified certificate of incorporators that no part of the capital has been paid, that business has not begun and that all rights and franchises are surrendered. (Sec. 38).

30b. Voluntary Dissolution After Business Has Begun is by a compliance with the provisions of section 39 of the corporation law; dissolution is effected by resolution of the directors calling a meeting of the stockholders on notice, and if two-thirds in interest of all stockholders signify their consent such consent is filed with the Secretary of State. The Secretary of State, if satisfied that a compliance with the law has been made, issues certificate of dissolution which must be duly published in a newspaper in the county where the principal office of the corporation is located in Delaware. Proof of publication thereof is filed with the Secretary of State and a copy of the certificate of dissolution recorded with the recorder of the proper county. (Sec. 39).

NOTE: The provisions of the statute in this regard should be very carefully studied and followed.

30c. **Continuation After Dissolution.** See No. 27c.

30d. **Directors Shall Become Trustees** upon voluntary dissolution with full power to liquidate and distribute assets. (Sec. 41).

30e. **Receivers** may be appointed by Court of Chancery. (Sec. 43).

31. INSOLVENCY

See No. 10 above.

VII. CORPORATE REORGANIZATION AND EXTENSION

32. RENEWAL OF CHARTER

32a. **Renewal Before Expiration of Time Limited for Existence** may be had by complying with the provisions of section 73 of the corporation law. The certificate setting forth the facts is filed with the Secretary of State.

NOTE: In practice nearly all of the corporations have charter provisions making their existence perpetual.

32b. **Such Renewal Certificate Shall Be Filed and Recorded** in the manner provided for original certificates of incorporation. (Sec. 74).

32c. **Corporations So Renewing Their Certificate of Incorporation** shall enjoy all the rights of the original certificate of incorporation as well as the benefits of the general corporation law. (Sec. 76).

33. CORPORATE REORGANIZATION

Upon the sale of corporate franchises and property of any corporation existing under the laws of Delaware, either at private sale or under judgment of the court, the purchasers may organize a corporation for the continuation, operation and management of such corporation with the same rights, privileges and franchises and subject to the limitations, restrictions and liabilities that attached to the original corporation. (Sec. 65).

VIII. FEES AND TAXES; DOMESTIC CORPORATIONS

34. FILING AND RECORDING FEES

Certificate of Incorporation.

The State Organization Tax is paid to the Secretary of State.

For each $1,000 of the total capital stock authorized up
    to $2,000,000...................................... $ .10

For each $1,000 of the total capital stock authorized above
    $2,000,000 .... .05

In no case less than 10.00
    Certificate of Increase.

And for each $1,000 of increase of capital stock, up to
    $2,000,000 of Increase (but in no case less than $5,00) $ .10

For each $1,000 increase above $2,000,000 of increase.. .05

NOTE: Upon increase of capital stock the tax of 10c per $1,000
is figured upon the first $2,000,000 new authorized stock, regardless
of the fact that the corporation may already have paid a state
organization tax at the 10c rate upon any part of $2,000,000 of
capital stock theretofore authorized.

CERTIFICATE OR AGREEMENT OF CONSOLIDATION OR MERGER

For each $1,000 of capital stock of new company, over and
    above the total capital stock of the companies so con-
    solidated or merged............................. $ .10

For each $1,000 above $2,000,000 .... .05
    Other State Fees.

Certificate of Dissolution (including the filing of all papers
    and issuing certificate under hand and seal of office).. $19.00

To publication of Certificate of Dissolution as required by
    Section 39 .... 3.50

Change of name, amended certificate of organization, de-
    crease of capital stock and increase or decrease of
    number of shares 10.00

Other certificates 5.00
    Fees to Secretary of State's Office.
    For Certified Copies:

Copying per line.................................... $ .02

For official seal on certificate 1.00

For receiving, filing and indexing any paper provided by
    law to be filed with him 2.00

No certified copy of Certificate of Incorporation less than $4.50.

NOTE: Certificates of incorporation must also be recorded with
the Recorder of the County where the principal office is located.
The charge usually ranges between $4.00 and $7.00.

35. FRANCHISE AND OTHER CORPORATE TAXES

35a. Annual Franchise Tax Based on Authorized Capital Stock:

Capitalization not exceeding $ 25,000	....	$5.00
Capitalization not exceeding 100,000	....	10.00
Capitalization not exceeding 300,000	....	20.00
Capitalization not exceeding 500,000	....	25.00
Capitalization not exceeding 1,000,000	....	50.00
For each additional million or part thereof	....	25.00

Any corporation showing by its annual report that it is not engaged in business shall pay one-half of the above, but not less than $5.00.

35b. Exemptions from Tax: Manufacturing or mining companies fifty per centum of whose capital stock issued and outstanding is invested in manufacturing and mining in this state. Such companies not having fifty per cent so invested may have deduction for amount invested. (Sec. 68 of Franchise Tax Act).

NOTE: Delaware is a particularly advantageous State for the organization of telegraph, telephone, cable, express companies, gas and electric light companies, heat and power companies, parlor, palace or sleeping car companies, or pipe line companies and certain other semi-public service corporations, owing to the fact that they are taxed upon their business in Delaware; therefore such corporations transacting their entire business without the State are exempt from the payment of the annual franchise tax. Such corporations should be careful to make reports upon the blanks provided by the Secretary of State covering the particular businesses, and not to report upon the business corporation blanks.

35c. There Is No Income Tax upon Corporations.
There is no State Stock Transfer Tax.
There Is No Inheritance Tax upon Non-residents.

NOTE: The Delaware Constitution, Art. 9, Section 6, provides: "Shares of the capital stock of corporations created under the laws of this State, when owned by persons or corporations without this State, shall not be subject to taxation by any law now existing or hereafter to be made".

IX. FOREIGN CORPORATIONS

36. RECOGNITION AND MANNER OF QUALIFYING TO DO BUSINESS

36a. No Corporation Shall Do Business in This State without having an authorized agent upon whom legal process may be served. (Const. Art. 9, sec. 5).

NOTE: The UNITED STATES CORPORATION COM-
PANY acts as agent for foreign corporations in Delaware and performs all of the duties of that office as well as for domestic corporations.

36b. **Each Foreign Corporation Must File** in the office of
the Secretary of State a certified copy of its certificate of incorporation, the name of its agent within this State, and a sworn statement
of assets and liabilities and pay a fee of $20.   (Sec. 188).

36c. **Certificate of Secretary of State** shall thereupon be
issued.   (Sec. 188).

36d. **Process** may be served on authorized agent.   (Sec. 191).

36e. **Change of Agent** may be made by filing certificate des-
ignating new agent, and in case of death or removal of agent,
corporation shall within ten days appoint an agent.   (Sec. 192).

NOTE: Naming The UNITED STATES CORPORATION
COMPANY as authorized agent furnishes a continuing service, and
the necessity for naming a new agent in case of death or removal,
etc., is overcome.

37. POWERS AND DUTIES OF FOREIGN CORPORATIONS

See Part 2 of this digest.

38. DOING BUSINESS WITHOUT AUTHORITY

38a. **Foreign Corporations or Agents** transacting business
within the State without authority shall be guilty of misdemeanor.
(Sec. 193).

39. FEES. TAXES AND REPORTS OF FOREIGN CORPORATIONS

39a. QUALIFYING FEES, State Tax, $10.00.   (Sec. 188).
For Secretary of State and the Prothonotaries, $10.00.

NOTE: The total entrance fee is $20.00.

39b. **There Are No Annual Taxes or Reports** due from foreign
corporations.

TAXES AND OFFICIAL FEES UPON INCORPORATION IN DELAWARE AND A SCHEDULE SHOWING COMPARATIVE COSTS IN MAINE, NEW JERSEY, ILLINOIS, NEW YORK, AND MISSOURI.

TABLE OF COMPARATIVE ORGANIZATION FEES AND ANNUAL TAXES

Capital	DELAWARE (Note No 1)		MAINE (Note No. 2)		NEW JERSEY (Note No. 3)	
	Organization Fees	Annual Tax	Organization Fees	Annual Tax	Organization Fees	Annual Tax
10,000	$10	$5	$10	$5	$25	$10
100,000	10	10	50	10	25	100
250,000	25	20	50	50	50	250
500,000	50	25	50	50	100	500
1,000,000	100	50	100	75	200	1,000
5,000,000	350	150	500	275	1,000	4,000
10,000,000	600	275	1,000	525	2,000	4,250
50,000,000	2,600	1,275	5,000	2,525	10,000	6,250
100,000,000	5,100	2,525	10,000	5,025	20,000	8,750

Capital	ILLINOIS (Note No. 4)		NEW YORK (Note No. 5)		MISSOURI (Note No. 6)	
	Organization Fees	Annual Tax	Organization Fees	Annual Tax	Organization Fees	Annual Tax
10,000	$20	$10	$10	$10	$50	$10
100,000	50	50	50	100	75	100
250,000	125	125	125	250	150	250
500,000	250	250	250	500	275	500
1,000,000	500	500	500	1,000	525	1,000
5,000,000	2,500	2,500	2,500	5,000	2,525	5,000
10,000,000	5,000	5,000	5,000	10,000	5,025	10,000
50,000,000	25,000	25,000	25,000	50,000	25,025	50,000
100,000,000	50,000	50,000	50,0C0	100,000	50,025	100,000

NOTE NO. 1. Based on authorized capital.

NOTE NO. 2. Based on authorized capital.

NOTE NO. 3. Organization tax based on authorized capital stock and annual tax based on issued capital stock.

NOTE NO. 4. Annual tax based on proportion of authorized capital represented by business transacted and property in state.

The figures here given cover total in state. Rate is 5c per $100.

NOTE NO. 5. Tax is at rate of $4\frac{1}{2}\%$ of income, or $1 per thousand based upon proportion of issued Capital stock, whichever is larger. The figures given represent minimum annual tax when all property is in state, and when all stock is issued.

NOTE NO. 6. Tax is at rate of one-tenth of 1% of outstanding capital stock represented by the proportion of capital stock and surplus apportioned to the state. Minimum tax, if all stock is issued and all property in Missouri is given. There is also an income tax in Missouri of $1\frac{1}{2}\%$ of income derived from business in Missouri.

In Delaware, Maine and Illinois, both the organization fees and annual franchise taxes, on shares without par value, are at the same rate as par value shares, an arbitrary value of $100 being fixed on each of such shares for these purposes only. In New York the organization tax on such shares is 5 cents per share and the franchise or income tax is paid on the proportion its capital within the state bears to its entire property.

In New Jersey the organization tax on such shares is 1 cent per share on authorized number of shares, with a minimum of $25; and the franchise tax is 3 cents on each share issued up to and including 20,000 shares, 2 cents on each of the next 10,000 of issued shares, 1 cent on each of the next 10,000 shares issued and $\frac{1}{4}$ of 1 cent on each issued share above 50,000 shares.

PART TWO

Being a Digest of the Decisions of the Supreme Court, the Court of Chancery and the Superior Court of Delaware, relating to the law regulating corporations.

The arrangement is the same as that of Part I. Each case is identified by a separate number combining the number of the section with the number given the particular case. Cases classified under one section are by these numbers cross referenced into other sections under which they may be sought.

1. THE CONSTITUTION

1-1. Const. 1897, art. 9, s. 6, providing that, in all elections for directors of stock corporations, each shareholder shall be entitled to one vote for each share of stock he may hold, provides that there shall be no discrimination between different classes of stock but provides generally that the holder of a share of stock is the holder of a vote, so that a holder of preferred stock is entitled to vote it, notwithstanding any statute authorizing corporations to create kinds of stock, with preferences and voting powers.—Brooks v. State, 79 A. 790. (Note: The section referred to is no longer a part of the Constitution.)

1-2. (Del. Super. 1909.) One may waive any provision of a statute or contract intended for his benefit. General Corporation Law (Laws 1901-03, p. 291, c. 167), s. 13, empowering every corporation to create two or more kinds of stock of such classes, with such designations, preferences and voting power or restrictions or qualifications thereto as shall be stated in the certificate of incorporation, gives the right to issue preferred stock without the right to vote, and the holders of such preferred stock waive the right to vote, notwithstanding Const. art. 9, s. 6, providing that in elections for directors each shareholder shall be entitled to one vote for each share of stock he may hold.—State v. Brooks, 74 A. 37. (Note Section referred to is no longer a part of the Constitution.)

See also Nos. 2-1, 3-5, 3-6, 8-4, 14-9, 14-10, 17-16, 23-6, 23-17, 24-1, 24-2, 24-3, 24-4, 24-12, 24-13, 29-2, 29-4.

2. THE STATUTES

2-1. A statute authorizing a corporation to give to its stock a voting power different from that prescribed by the Constitution is void.—Brooks v. State, 79 A. 790.

2-2. 20 Laws, c. 513, requiring foreign corporation to file certificate, etc., held not to apply to the contracts of corporations made before its passage.—Standard Sewing-Mach. Co. v. Frame. (Del. Super.) 48 A. 188.

2-3. (Del. 1904). Under General Corporation Law 1901, s. 3, (22 Del. Laws, p. 287, c. 167), providing that the act shall apply to every corporation so far as "necessary or convenient" to the attainment of the objects set forth in its charter, the certificate required by section 23 in any case of payment on capital stock is not inconsistent with the charter of a corporation providing for a certificate in case of any increase of its capital stock, so as to render section 23 (22 Del. Laws, p. 294, c. 167) inapplicable to such corporation.—Bay State Gas Co. v. State, 56 A. 1120, 4 Pennewill, 497.

2-4. (Del.) Each sovereignty held to have authority to exclude corporations created by another sovereignty or to prescribe terms with which they must comply.—Model Heating Co. v. Magarity, 81 A. 394, 2 Boyce, 459, L.R.A. 1915B, 665.

See also Nos. 3-2, 3-3, 3-4, 3-5, 3-6, 6-9, 8-4, 10-6, 10-12, 10-13, 10-21, 10-24, 14-9, 14-31, 15-1, 17-13, 17-16, 23-1, 23-4, 23-6, 23-15, 24-1, 24-2, 24-3, 24-11, 25-1, 29-2, 29-3, 31-20, 31-48, 31-57.

3. CORPORATE CHARTERS AND ORGANIZATION OF CORPORATIONS

3-1. The fiction of a legal corporate entity will be ignored, when used to shield fraudulent or illegal acts.—Martin v. D. B. Martin Co., 88 A. 612.

3-2. A provision in the charter of a corporation, which gives to its stock a voting power different from that contemplated by the statute under which it is created, is void.—Brooks v. State, 79 A. 790.

3-3. A mere act of incorporation cannot of itself create an existing corporation in point of fact. It does not create but only authorizes. It must afterward be organized and established, in order to give it any life as a corporation.—P., W. & B. R. R. Co. v. Kent Co. R. R. Co., 5 Houst. 127 (132, 133).

3-4. An express acceptance of an act of incorporation is not essential to the corporate existence unless so required by the act. An acceptance will be implied from an organization of incorporators and the exercise of corporate powers.—Logan v. McAllister, 2 Del. Ch. 176 (186).

3-5. The provisions of Const. 1831, art. 2, s. 17, became a part of the charter of corporations subsequently formed, and the legislature may exert the power therein given at any time.—Wilmington City Ry. Co. v. Wilmington & B. S. Ry. Co. (Del. Ch.) 46 A. 12.

3-6. The organization of corporations, created by special law after the adoption of Const. art. 9, s. 1, providing that no corporation shall be created by special, but only by general, law, is not within such constitutional inhibition.—State v. Hancock (Del. Super.) 45 A. 851.

See also Nos. 2-3, 6-22, 23-14, 24-2, 24-3, 24-4, 25-1.

4. AMENDMENT OF CORPORATE CHARTERS

4-1. An amendment or supplement to the charter of a company is not an act of incorporation, unless it confers additional rights and franchises, and hence does not require the concurrence of both branches of the Legislature, unless the act confers additional rights and franchises of a corporate nature, or confirms rights already existing in the company.—Bailey v. P., W. & B. R. R. Co., 4 Harr. 389 (416).
See also No. 14-5.

5. MERGER AND CONSOLIDATION OF CORPORATIONS

5-1. (Del. Ch.) Mining company's exchange of its mining property and assets, except treasury stock, etc., for shares of another mining company, held not a consolidation or merger with such other company.—Butler v. New Keystone Copper Co., 93 A. 380.

6. CORPORATE MEETINGS AND ELECTIONS

6a. Corporate Elections.

6-1. An election of directors, at which stock was voted which was transferred to the voter within 20 days prior thereto, is void.—In re Vernon (Del. Super.) 4 A. 60.

6-2. (Del. Ch.). Under General Corporation Act s. 9., providing that directors shall each own three shares of stock, person who became assignee of incorporator's subscription to capital stock became eligible to election as a director.—Lippman v. Kehoe Stenograph Co. 98 A. 943. (Note: Act s. 9 now amended removing this requirement.)

6-3. Stockholder who assigned certificate in blank without sale and delivered with no intention of either party that his interest should terminate, no transfer being made on books of company, was not disqualified to be a director under General Corporation Law, s. 9.—Lippman v. Kehoe Stenograph Co., 98 A. 943.

6-4. When ownership of shares in a corporation is necessary to qualify as a director, a party who sells and assigns his shares disqualifies himself.—Lippman v. Kehoe Stenograph Co., 98 A. 943.

6-5. In corporations aggregate, where the principle of election is not specified in the charter, it requires a majority of the corporators voting to elect to office; contrary in this respect to the plurality principle which governs in all elections in this State.—State v. Wil. City Council, 3 Harr. 294, (300).

6-6. If the term of an office is not limited to expire at a fixed time, or upon a specified event, but there is simply a direction for the annual election of the officer, his original term continues, though after the year, until a successor is duly elected and qualified.—Sparks v. Farmers Bank, 3 Del. Ch. 274 (296).

6-7. Notice must be served on the corporation of an application to set aside its election of directors, as provided in Rev. Code, p. 579, s. 24.—In re Vernon (Del. Super.) 60.

6-8. A rule to show cause why petition to set aside an election of directors should not be granted need not be issued where notice of such application was given.—In re Vernon (Del. Super.) 40 A. 60.

6-9. (Del. Super. 1904). Act March 14, 1883 (17 Del. Laws, p. 225, c. 147), s. 24, providing that the superior court, on application of any person aggrieved by any corporate election, after hearing, may order a new election, or make such order as to right and justice may appertain, does not apply to corporations created under the general corporation law, approved March 10, 1899 (21 Del. Laws, P. 445, c. 273), as amended by Acts 1901.—In re Powell, 58 A. 831.

6-10. (Del. Ch.) Directors of a corporation having permitted the time for the holding of the annual meeting for the election of directors to pass without such election, petitioner, a majority stockholder, held entitled to a summary order of the chancellor requiring the holding of such election under Laws 1901-03, c. 394.—In re Jackson, 81 A. 992, 9 Del. Ch. 279.

6-11. (Del. Ch.) Judges of election of directors of corporation held to have improperly refused to allow another corporation, holder of shares in first, to vote at election on ground it represented shares transferred within 20 days.—In re Election of Directors of Associated Automatic Sprinkler Co., 102 A. 787.

6-12. Statute of Pennsylvania, not invalidating new certificates of stock, where tax imposed on transfer of shares has not been paid, had no bearing on right of one corporation holding stock in another to vote for directors of such other after having assigned 12 of its 2,013 shares previous to election, taking new certificate for 2,001 shares.—In re Election of Directors of Associated Automatic Sprinkler Co., 102 A. 787.

6-13. Falsity of list of stockholders in one corporation, prepared for and exhibited at meeting to elect directors, held not to deprive other corporation, stockholder in first, of right to vote its stock.—In re Election of Directors of Associated Automatic Sprinkler Co., 102 A. 787.

6-14. Where corporation, stockholder in another, has wrongfully been excluded from voting its stock at election of directors, facts being simple and rights involved clear, Court of Chancery can grant relief (1) by correcting return of election to accord with legal rights of stockholder, corporation, (2) by ordering new election, and (3) by ordering officers of corporation and judges of election to correct return.—In re Election of Directors of Associated Automatic Sprinkler Co., 102 A. 787.

See also Nos. 1-1 1-2, 2-1, 3-2, 13-4, 17-16, 19-2.

6b. **Corporate Meetings.**

6-15. Under General Corporation Law, s. 3 and section 5, par. 8, and s. 32 held that, where certificate of incorporation so provides, directors' meetings may be held outside the state.—Lippman v. Kehoe Stenograph Co., 95 A. 895.

6-16. (Del. Ch.) Directors of a corporation who were stockholders before they acted as directors were qualified to act as such, though not so qualified when elected.—Lippman v. Kehoe Stenograph Co., 95 A. 895.

6-17. Directors' meeting of which all eligible directors had notice, and which was attended by a quorum of such directors, held valid, notwithstanding presence of persons disqualified and never elected.—Lippman v. Kehoe Stenograph Co., 95 A. 895.

6-18. (Del. Ch.) Signature of third director, not present at alleged meeting, to false minutes made up by other two directors and initialed by them, was ineffective, unless subsequently ratified at valid meeting.—Lippman v. Kehoe Stenograph Co., 98 A. 943.

6-19. Where one of three directors believed the minutes of an alleged meeting, at which he had not been present, and their validity, to be conditional on subsequent ratification at another meeting, their validity was conditional.—Lippman v. Kehoe Stenograph Co., 98 A. 943.

6-20. Directors of corporation were not estopped to deny validity of alleged directors' meeting, or to repudiate it, where such meeting was not legally held, and the minutes thereof, concocted by two of the three directors, were signed by the directors with knowledge of their falsity.—Lippman v. Kehoe Stenograph Co., 98 A. 943.

6-21. Where incorporators elected six directors by ballot, three of whom were ineligible because not stockholders, a directors' meeting of two of the three eligible directors, pursuant to notice to all, was valid, despite presence of ineligible members.—Lippman v. Kehoe Stenograph Co., 98 A. 943.

6-22. (Del. Ch.) Provision of General Corporation Act, s. 32, that directors may hold meetings outside state if by-laws so provide, does not apply, where, in certificate of incorporation, right to hold meetings outside state is taken as authorized by sections 3 and 5, paragraph 8.—Lippman v. Kehoe Stenograph Co., 98 A. 943.

6-23. Court of equity should not invalidate proceedings of directors at a meeting outside the state when every stockholder and director had notice of the place, and either attended or failed to object that place was outside state.—Lippman v. Kehoe Stenograph Co., 98 A. 943.

6-24. In general, directors may hold meetings and transact business outside state wherein company is incorporated, unless otherwise prescribed by charter or by-laws.—Lippman v. Kehoe Stenograph Co., 98 A. 943.

6-25. (Del. Ch.) Act of director in signing, before organization of company, blank form of waiver of notice to him of directors' meetings was insufficient to validate, as against other stockholder or director, meeting subsequently held, at which he was not present and of which he had no notice.—Lippman v. Kehoe Stenograph Co., 98 A. 943.

6-26. Where less than four months after election persons elected as directors acquired requisite number of shares and entered upon discharge of their duties, they are qualified though not owners of required shares at time of election.—Lippman v. Kehoe Stenograph Co., 102 A. 988.

6-27. (Del.) Despite Code 1915, s. 1946, directors' meeting held outside state is valid under sections 1917, 1919, where certificate of incorporation provided that directors' meetings might be held outside state, though there was no by-law so providing.—Lippman v. Kehoe Stenograph Co., 102 A. 988.

6-28. (Del.) Where no directors' meeting in fact was had, purported minutes of such meeting prepared and signed by some of directors are of no force.—Lippman v. Kehoe Stenograph Co., 102 A. 988.

6-29. (Del.) In suit against corporation and officers to enjoin alleged illegal forfeiture of stock, question of election and qualifications of directors may be determined by chancellor.—Lippman **v.** Kehoe Stenograph Co., 102 A. 988.

6-30. In such suit, question of legality of meeting of board of directors held without state of corporations domicile is proper one for determination by chancellor.—Lippman v. Kehoe Stenograph Co., 102 A. 988.

6-31. In such suit, held, that stockholder could not attack action of directors on ground that no one of them as required by statute of corporation's domicile was resident of state.—Lippman v. Kehoe Stenograph Co., 102 A. 988.

6-32. (Del. Ch.) Special directors' meeting of which absent director had no notice and did not waive notice held invalid, though he subsequently signed the minutes and a waiver of notice.—Lippman v. Kehoe Stenograph Co., 95 A. 895.

6-33. (Del. Ch.) Meeting of incorporators to organize corporation under General Corporation Law, sec. 8, held valid, when acquiesced in, though two of the incorporators acted by proxy.—Lippman v. Kehoe Stenograph Co., 95 A. 895.

See also Nos. 19-11, 19-12, 19-13.

7. CORPORATE MANAGEMENT AND CORPORATE BUSINESS

7-1. Neither words of in testimonium, nor reference to the seal at all, are necessary to the validity of an instrument under seal of a corporation.—Conine v. J. & B. R. R. Co., 3 Houst. 288 (298).

7-2. (Del. Ch. 1910) A provision, in a corporate mortgage to secure bonds, that written notice must be delivered to the president, secretary, and treasurer of the corporation at its principal office to make overdue payments within 30 days, as a condition precedent to foreclosure, is complied with where the president, secretary, and treasurer in fact received the notice, though it was not delivered to them at the principal office of the corporation, where the corporation had consolidated with another corporation, and so had no principal office.—Real Estate Trust Co. of Philadelphia v. Wilmington & N. C. Electric Ry. Co., 77 A. 756.

See also Nos. 6-13, 6-15, 6-27, 6-28, 8-8, 10-10, 10-15, 10-16, 11-8, 14-27, 23-18, 31-16, 31-21, 31-23, 31-27.

8. CORPORATION BOOKS, NOTICES AND RECORDS

8a. Inspection of Books.

8-1. (Del. Super.) A stockholder has the right to inspect the books of the corporation at a proper time for proper purposes.—State v. United Brokerage Co., 101 A. 433.

8-2. Corporation books are evidence in a suit between the company and a corporator.—Jefferson v. Stewart, 4 Harr. 82 (83).

8-3. Corporation's books not being open to the public, failure to record assignment of stock as collateral security held not to render such assignment void as to creditors.—Allen v. Stewart (Del. Ch.) 44 A. 786.

8-4. (Del. 1904.) General Corporation Law 1901, s. 29 (22 Del. Laws, p. 298, c. 167), requiring the original or duplicate stock ledgers of corporations to be kept open to the examination of stockholders, is applicable to a domestic corporation organized prior to the Constitution of the state in force at the time of the passage of the act, though such corporation had never had its charter amended under the act, or filed an acceptance of the provisions of the Constitution.—Bay State Gas Co. v. State, 56 A. 1114, 4 Pennewill, 238.

8-5. (Del. 1909.) That corporate books are in another state is no defense to an alternative writ of mandamus to produce such books for inspection.—State v. Jessup & Moore Paper Co., 72 A. 1057, 7 Pennewill, 397.

8-6. Corporate books and papers should not be subject to unnecessary, unreasonable, or untimely inspection, and when a stockholder demands the right to inspect the same the directors are entitled to have the assurance that the information sought is not for the purpose of injuring the corporate business, or building up a rival concern, or any other improper purpose.—State v. Jessup & Moore Paper Co., 72 A. 1057, 7 Pennewill, 397.

8-7. (Del. 1910.) The Superior Court can compel a domestic corporation to produce books in the possession of its officers outside the state.—State v. Jessup & Moore Paper Co., 77 A. 16.

8-8. (Del. Ch.) Certain subsidiary corporations, whose stock was substantially owned by defendant corporation, and whose directors and principal officers were practically the same as defendant's, held mere instrumentalities of defendant, so that, in a suit by defendant's stockholders to compel it to produce the corporate books for discovering whether it was fraudulently mismanaging its corporate affairs, defendant will be compelled to produce the books of such companies, as well as its own.—Martin v. D. B. Martin Co., 88 A. 612.

8-9. (Del. Super.) A stockholder may not compel a corporation to submit to an examination of its books and papers, where his motive is to institute harassing litigation against the corporation to compel it to purchase the stockholder's shares.—State v. Jessup & Moore Paper Co., 88 A. 449, 4 Boyce, 248.

8-10. Failure of relator to vote at a stockholders' meeting, to attend at another meeting at which the corporation's general ledger was opened to inspection, and to co-operate in the corporation's efforts partially to comply with a decision with reference to an examination of its books, held not to show that relator's application for that purpose was made in bad faith or pursuant to an improper motive.—State v. Jessup & Moore Paper Co., 88 A. 449, 4 Boyce, 248.

See also Nos. 13-3, 17-10, 17-11, 31-7, 31-22, 37-7.

8b. **Notices, etc.**

8-11. Notice to an authorized agent or officer of a corporation, such as a president, binds the principal.—Newport Nat. Bank v. Tweed, 4 Houst. 225 (232).

See also Nos. 7-2, 10-20, 10-21.

9. CORPORATION REPORTS

9-1. (Del. Gen. Sess.) General Incorporation Law, s. 152, (applicable to railroads only) making it misdemeanor for corporation to fail to file annual report applies to corporation created by special act prior to passage of the General Incorporation Act, especially in view of Const. art. 9, s. 1, 2, 4, and General Incorporation Law, s. 3. —State v. Front & Union St. Ry. Co., 104 A. 154.

10. COURTS, COURT PROCEDURE, PLEADING AND EVIDENCE

10a. **Legal Actions.**

10-1. Civil corporations, whether public or private, are subject to the general law of the land, and amenable to the judicial tribunals for the proper exercise of their powers.—State v. Wil. City Council, 3 Harr. 294 (299).

10-2. (Del. Super.) Action for damages for fraudulent representations by defendants in sale of mining stock to plaintiff in Pennsylvania was governed by law of that state in so far as applicable to facts.—Williams v. Beltz, 101 A. 905.

10-3. (Del. Super.) Measure of damages for false representation of material fact affecting value of mining stock is difference between real value of stock at time of purchase and what purchaser was induced to pay by reason of misrepresentation.—Williams v. Beltz, 101 A. 905.

10-4. In a suit to cancel stock unlawfully issued, where the appointment of a receiver pendente lite was sought to preserve the property of the corporation, a court of equity can give that relief, where the corporation is before the court and the stockholders whose stock is sought to be canceled filed affidavits and had actual notice of the proceedings, though not served with the rule for the appointment of the receiver.—Ellis v. Penn Beef Co., 80 A. 666.

10-5. (Del. Ch.) Where a company in process of dissolution has, prior to appointment of a receiver, broken its executory contract, injured party is not deprived of his rights to a remedy for the breach as against assets in hands of receiver.—Fell v. Securities Co. of North America, 97 A. 610.

10-6. (Del. Super. 1902.) Objection that a suit to hold a local stockholder in a foreign corporation liable for the corporation debts could not be maintained, because in form an action of debt, and not on the case, and in such respect and others not in conformity with General Incorporation Act, s. 49 (Laws 1899, c. 273), and other provisions of the act, was untenable; the provisions referring only to domestic corporations.—Love v. Pusey & Jones Co., 52 A. 542, 3 Pennewill, 577.

10-7. (Del. Super. 1902.) A Delaware stockholder in a Kansas corporation may be held liable in suit in Delaware for debts of the corporation, pursuant to constitutional and statutory provisions of Kansas.—Love v. Pusey & Jones Co., 52 A. 542 '3 Pennewill, 577.

10-8. The fact that petitioners would be primarily liable for the expense of litigation against officers and directors of a corporation for alleged mismanagement, and that delay and loss of evidence would be avoided, and that the company's receiver was not entirely favorable to the suit, was not ground for the granting of permission to petitioning stockholders to institute and maintain the action.—Du Pont v. Standard Arms Co., 82 A. 692, 9 Del. Ch. 324.

10-9. In a suit to enjoin officers and agents of a corporation from laying gas pipes in a street, the corporation is a necessary defendant.—City of Wilmington v. Addicks (Del. Ch.) 43 A. 297.

10-10. (Del. Ch. 1910.) A sale under foreclosure of a mortgage of a corporation to secure its bonds was made for $10,000 to the only bidder, who acted as trustee for the holders of 95 per cent. of the bonds. The holder of 5 per cent. of the bonds refused to join the other bondholders, and he objected to a confirmation of the sale on the ground of inadequacy of the price, and averred that on a resale an unnamed purchaser would probably bid $20,000. There was evidence that the property was worth $30,000. Held that, where there was no fraud or irregularity, the court in its discretion must confirm the sale.—Central Trust & Savings Co. v. Chester County Electric Co., 77 A. 771.

See also Nos. 3-1, 6-9, 6-14, 6-29, 6-31, 8-2, 8-5, 8-7, 8-8, 9-1, 11-3, 11-4, 11-5, 13-2, 14-2, 14-8, 14-13, 14-15, 14-30, 14-31, 17-3, 17-4, 17-5, 17-22, 19-4, 19-6, 19-7, 20-2, 23-13, 23-14, 29-1, 31-11, 31-13, 31-29, 31-37, 31-57, 31-60, 31-62, 37-4, 37-6.

10b. **Service of Notice and of Process.**

10-11. (Del. Gen. Sess.) In view of Rev. Code 1852, amended to

1893, p. 702, c. 94, sec. 3, empowering the judges of the Court of General Sessions to issue writs to take any person indicted, and the general corporation law, providing that legal process may be served on corporations as therein provided, held, that a capias would issue against an indicted corporation to be served as a writ of summons.— State v. Charles M. Scott Packing Co., 89 A. 369, 4 Boyce, 517.

10-12. By doing business in Delaware by branch establishment or regular agency, a nonresident does not assent to service of process on him in Delaware in the manner prescribed by its laws, regardless of their constitutionality.—Caldwell v. Armour (Del. Super.) 43 A. 517.

10-13. Under Act March 23, 1871, as amended April 25, 1889, there can be no garnishment of a nonresident corporation without service of process on the officers named therein.—National Bank of Wilmington and Brandywine v. Furtick (Del. Err. & App.) 42 A. 479.

10-14. (Del. Ch. 1910.) In a suit against a corporation, personal service of process on three persons, forming a part of the board of nine directors, of which complainant is one, is insufficient service on the corporation.—Thoroughgood v. Georgetown Water Co., 77 A. 720.

10-15. (Del. Super. 1910.) A motion to set aside service of a summons on a person as president of defendant corporation, on the ground that he is not its president, should disclose who the president is, or some other officer on whom service may be had, or show that there is no such officer.—Arnold v. Sentinel Printing Co., 77 A. 966.

10-16. The petition of the manager of defendant corporation to set aside service of summons on W. as its president, supported by W.'s affidavit that he is not and was not its president, and the manager's affidavit that he does not know who are its president and directors, and that to the best of his knowledge and belief there are none, should be granted, unless plaintiff satisfies the court that such statements are untrue.—Arnold v. Sentinel Printing Co., 77 A. 966.

10-17. (Del. Ch. 1910.) A general appearance for a corporation by its solicitor cures insufficient service of process, served personally on three persons forming a part of the board of directors.— Thoroughgood v. Georgetown Water Co., 77 A. 720.

10-18. (Del. Super. 1909.) In garnishment proceedings in which a corporation is made garnishee, summons must be served personally upon those officers designated by statute.—Fowler v. Dickson, 74 A. 601.

10-19. (Del. Ch. 1910.) An answer by three persons, forming a part of the board of directors of a corporation, personally served with process in a suit against the corporation, which does not purport to be the answer of the corporation, but of the three directors, and which alleges that the other directors are nonresidents, and that they have the books of the corporation, is not an answer of the corporation, and on the expiration of the time for answering, complainant may move for a decree pro confesso against the corporation.—Thoroughgood v. Georgetown Water Co., 77 A. 720.

10-20. (Del. 1904.) General Corporation Law 1901, s. 48 (22 Del. Laws, p. 305, c. 167), provides that service of legal process upon "any corporation created under this act," on the president of the corporation, by copy left at his dwelling house or usual place of abode, to be effective, must be delivered thereat at least six days before return of the process. Section 3 makes the act applicable to all corporations of the state, without regard to when they were organized. Held, that service of the rule and alternative writ in mandamus proceedings by stockholders of the corporation to obtain inspection of the books, by delivering a copy at the residence in the state, six days before the return day thereof, of the president of a domestic corporation organized prior to the taking effect of the Constitution of the State in force at the time of the passage of the act, is sufficient, though the president was not in fact within the state.—Bay State Gas Co. v. State, 56 A. 1114, 4 Pennewill, 238.

10-21. (Del. Super. 1901.) A return of service of rule to show cause why mandamus should not issue to compel a corporation to keep its books open for the inspection of stockholders, stating that service of the rule was made on defendant corporation by leaving a copy thereof, together with a copy of the petition and affidavits, at the dwelling house of the president of the company on a given date, at least six days before the return day thereof, in the presence of a certain white adult person, and also that service was made on defendant president of the company in the same manner, was sufficient, under General Corporation Act 1901 (22 Del. Laws, p. 305, c. 167), s. 48, providing for service of process against corporations at least six days before the return of the process, at the usual place of abode or principal office of the corporation.—State v. Bay State Gas Co., 57 A. 291, 4 Pennewill, 214.

10-22. (Del. Super. 1901.) A similar return of the service of the alternative writ of mandamus was likewise sufficient.—State v. Bay State Gas Co., 57 A. 291, 4 Pennewill, 214.

10-23. (Del. Super. 1901.) Under General Corporation Act 1901 (22 Del. Laws, p. 305, c. 167), s. 48, providing for service of process on corporations by copy left at the principal office or place of business at least six days before the return of the process, there must be six days exclusive of the return of service.—State v. Bay State Gas Co., 57 A. 291, 4 Pennewill, 214.

10b. 6-7, 6-8, 6-10.

-10c. **Pleadings and Procedure.**

10-24. (Del.) Creditor's remedy by "bill in chancery" against a stockholder of a corporate debtor, given by General Corporation Law (22 Del. Laws, c. 394), s. 49, must be initiated by a creditors' bill.—Du Pont v. Ball, 106 A. 39.

10-25. (Del. Super.) A corporation defendant is sufficiently identified by pleading its name, though the prefix "the" was omitted from the name.—Culver v. Philadelphia, B. & W. R. Co., 102 A. 980.

10-26. Under rules of court of chancery, answer of corporation is complete without affidavit, there being no rule of court providing specifically by what officer or how an affidavit shall be made in such case.—Whitmer v. William Whitmer & Sons, 98 A. 940.

10-27. (Del. Super.) Affidavit of demand in an action by a corporation on a book account held insufficient, because the treasurer did not swear therein that he was the treasurer of plaintiff corporation. Wilmington Sash & Door Co. v. Taylor, 82 A. 86, 2 Boyce, 528.

10-28. (Del. Super. 1902.) Debt was the proper form of action where it was sought to hold a local stockholder in a foreign corporation liable for the corporation's debts, pursuant to the statutory and constitutional provisions of the foreign state.—Love v. Pusey & Jones Co., 52 A. 542, 3 Pennewill, 577.

10-29. Where a mortgagee proceeds by scire facias, and afterwards by a bill in equity under which the property was sold, he cannot recover costs in the first proceeding.—Van Vrankin v. Roberts (Del. Ch.) 29 A. 1044.

10-30. An objection that a foreign corporation has not complied with certain statutory requirements cannot be sustained, unless raised by plea in abatement, special plea, or answer.—Standard Sewing-Mach. Co. v. Frame. (Del. Super.) 48 A. 188.

10-31. Covenant will not lie either against the president personally or against the company where the president of an incorporated company which has no seal, executes articles of agreement as president, under his hand, and a common scroll for a seal, but if it was done with the sanction and consent of the company the company might be liable in another form of action.—McCaulley v. Jenney, 5 Houst. 32 (33, 34).

See also Nos. 11-2, 11-6, 11-7, 23-5, 23-12, 24-5, 24-6, 31-49, 36-1, 37-2, 37-8.

10d. **Evidence.**

10-32. (Del. Super. 1910.) Under Rev. Code 1852, amended to 1893, p. 791, c. 106, s. 6, providing that, in any action by or against a corporation, it shall not be necessary for plaintiff on the trial to prove the incorporation, but this shall be taken to be admitted as alleged on the record unless defendant file, on or before the time of filing the plea in the action, an affidavit denying the existence of the corporation as alleged, before a judgment can be granted to a plaintiff corporation upon an affidavit of demand, that the plaintiff is a corporation and the place of its creation should appear, either in the title of the suit or in the affidavit of demand.—C. J. Toerring Co. v. R. E. Moore Co., 75 A. 786.

See also Nos. 13-1, 24-7, 31-50.

11. NAME AND SEAL

11a. **Name.**

11-1. (Del. Ch.) The similarity of names of complainant, Oklahoma Producing & Refining Company, and defendant, Oklahoma Consolidated Producing & Refining Company, being such that the public would probably be deceived thereby, tending naturally to harm complainant, complainant is entitled to have its rights protected by preliminary injunction against defendant's use of its name until the case can be fully heard upon the proofs adduced in the regular way.—Oklahoma Producing & Refining Co. v. Oklahoma Consol. Producing & Refining Co., 106 A. 38.

11-2. (Del. Super. 1903.) The use of the word "the" in a declaration before the title of defendant corporation, where defendant's true title contains no "the", is a misnomer, which renders the declaration obnoxious to a plea in abatement.—Lapham v. Philadelphia B. & W. R. Co., 56 A. 366, 4 Pennewill, 421.

11-3. (Del. Super. 1902.) When, in a suit involving a mechanic's lien against a corporation, it has been sued under a name which it has ceased to be known by, the corporation may appear specially and file an affidavit of defense; but such affidavit must show that the corporation is using a name different from that which it was sued under, and the necessary facts connected therewith.—Montello Brick Co. v. Pullman's Palace Car Co., 54 A. 687, 4 Pennewill, 90.

See also Nos. 10-25, 37-5.

11b. **Seal.**

11-4. When the common seal of a corporation appears to be affixed to an instrument, and the signature of a proper officer is proved or admitted, the court is bound to presume that the officer did not exceed his authority and the seal is prima facie evidence that the seal was affixed with proper authority; and, although it m ay be controverted, the burden of proof rests on the party objecting to it.—Conine v. J. & B. R. R. Co., 3 Houst. 288 (296, 297).

11-5. Where, in an action on a corporation's note, no corporate seal appears on the copy of the note annexed to the affidavit of demand, the note is insufficient.—St. Joseph's Polish Catholic Beneficial Soc. v. St. Hedwig's Church. (Del. Super.) 50 A. 535.

11-6. (Del. Ch.) A corporation, in respect to answering a bill in equity, speaks by its corporate seal.—Whitmer v. William Whitmer & Sons, 98 A. 940.

11-7. (Del. Ch.) Where corporation answers under its corporate seal, authenticity of seal must be established by attestation of proper officer.—Hopper v. Fesler Sales Co., 100 A. 791.

11-8. A seal is no more necessary to render valid the acts and contracts of a corporation, than of an individual; and in all cases where a natural person would be bound without a seal, a corporation will also be bound.—Derringer's Admr. v. Derringer's Admr., 5 Houst. 416 (427); Bancroft v. Wil. Conf. Acad., 5 Houst. 577 (579 et. seq.); Vandergrift v. Del. R. R. Co., 2 Houst. 287 (298).

See also Nos. 7-1, 10-31.

12. LEGAL DOMICILE AND PLACE OF BUSINESS

No decision.

13. BY-LAWS

13-1. The by-laws of a corporation are evidence against its officers, though they be not members of the corporation.—Bank of Wil. & B. v. Wollaston, 3 Harr. 90 (91).

13-2. The court cannot presume a corporate by-law, although upon an issue of fact depending before them they may instruct the jury to find one, upon evidence of long and ancient usage.—State v. Wil. City Council, 3 Harr. 294 (300).

13-3. (Del. 1910.) A corporate by-law, making inspection of books by a stockholder discretionary with the directors and prohibiting the making of extracts, is illegal and void.—State v. Jessup & Moore Paper Co., 77 A. 16.

13-4. (Del. 1911.) A by-law of a corporation, that restricts or alters the voting power of stock of a corporation as established by the law of its charter, is void.—Brooks v. State, 79 A. 790.

See also Nos. 14-33, 25-3.

14. STOCK, CAPITAL, CAPITAL STOCK

14a. Value and Voting Power of Stock.

14-1. Preferred stockholders could not be denied relief in suit to cancel common stock issued for a valueless consideration, because they acquired their stock subsequent to the unlawful issue.—Scully v. Automobile Finance Co., 101 A. 908.

14-2. (Del. Ch.) In a stockholder's suit to cancel stock issued for a valueless consideration, terms to protect and enforce all rights may be imposed in granting relief.—Scully v. Automobile Finance Co., 101 A. 908.

14-3. Representation by seller of mining stock that company's liabilities were $1,600, without disclosing contract under which it subsequently paid him $36,000 out of net profits, was misrepresentation of fact, affecting value of stock.—Williams v. Beltz, 101 A. 905.

See also Nos. 10-2, 10-3, 13-4, 31-31.

14b. **Stock Subscriptions and Payment for Stock.**

14-4. (Del. Ch.) Where directors for incorporating services and services to be performed issued corporate stock of value greatly in excess of value of such services, innocent purchaser for value who took shares is exempt from liability to pay any part of par value.— John W. Cooney Co. v. Arlington Hotel Co., 101 A. 879.

14-5. If the subscriber to stock enters into a corporation generally without specific stipulations, he is bound and concluded by the action of a majority of the corporation; and if the Legislature amends and changes the charter with the assent of the company, he will not thereby be discharged from his liability for subscription for stock, made previous to the change of the charter, unless the subscription is of such a character or the charge is of such a nature that it would increase the amount which he was originally bound to pay.—Del. R. R. Co. v. Tharp, 1 Houst. 149 (174 et seq).

14-6. (Del. Ch.) Agreement between corporation and its stockholders that corporate stock should be issued otherwise than for money paid or statutory equivalent is void, and agreement that common stock should be issued as bonus to purchasers of preferred stock is invalid.—John W. Cooney Co. v. Arlington Hotel Co., 101 A. 879.

14-7. (Del. Ch.) Issue of nearly $3,000,000 worth of common stock for promotion services and services to be rendered in disposing of preferred stock is fraudulent within General Corporation Law, Sec. 14, and Const. art. 9, Sec. 3, and may be attacked by corporate creditors.—John W. Cooney Co. v. Arlington Hotel Co., 101 A. 879.

14-8. (Del. Ch.) Contract authorizing outsider to take shares of stock in insurance company at par held not subject to attack as oppressive.—Kingston v. Home Life Ins. Co. of America, 101 A. 898.

14-9. (Del. Ch.) Constitutional and statutory prohibitions respecting issue of stock except for property do not prohibit issue of stock as partly paid for, but require it to be actually paid for, if issued as fully paid.—Scully v. Automobile Finance Co., 101 A. 908.

14-10. (Del. Ch.) Under General Corporation Law, Sec. 14, and

Const. art. 9, Sec. 3, corporate stock cannot be issued for promotion services or work to be done.—John W. Cooney Co. v. Arlington Hotel Co., 101 A. 879.

14-11. (Del. Ch.) Purchasers of preferred stock who received common stock as bonus cannot question validity of issue of preferred stock on ground that it was issued in violation of General Corporation Law, Sec. 13, declaring that at no time shall it exceed two-thirds of actual capital paid in cash or property.—John W. Cooney Co. v. Arlington Hotel Co., 101 A. 879.

Law not now in force in Delaware.

14-12. (Del. Ch. 1911.) Where a stock subscription was made at a premium, and the contract required each stockholder to pay the entire premium before payments should be applied to the shares, and entitled him to a certificate only after paying both premium and par value, upon dissolution, stockholders who have fully paid the premium and par value should share proportionately with those who have paid the premium and a part of the par value; the latter only sharing to the extent of payments upon the par value.—Grone v. Economic Life Ins. Co., 80 A. 809.

14-13. (Del. Ch.) Where an unauthorized agent sold stock, and the contract was ratified by the delivery of property of the corporation to the buyer and bringing suit for specific performance, the contract was enforceable by the seller.—U. S. Fire Apparatus Co. v. G. W. Baker Mach. Co., 95 A. 294.

14-14. A purchaser of stock need only look to the title of his vendor on the books of the company, and is not affected by previous irregularity in the transfers.—S. C., 1 Harr. 44 (45, 47).

14-15. Where the terms of the subscription contain no promise to pay, and the charter only authorizes a forfeiture of stock for nonpayment, no action will lie on a stock subscription.—Odd Fellows Hall Co. v. Glazier, 5 Harr. 172 (172 et seq).

14-16. (Del. Ch.) Defendant, who contracted to buy stock to acquire a patent, having opportunity for inspection, there being no deception, could not rescind because of third person's threat to sue for infringement.—U. S. Fire Apparatus Co. v. G. W. Baker Mach. Co., 95 A. 294.

14-17. (Del. Ch.) In action for breach of contract to buy stock, measure of damages is difference between market value at time of breach and contract price.—U. S. Fire Apparatus Co. v. G. W. Baker Mach. Co., 95 A. 294.

14-18. Those subsequently acquiring corporate stock cannot complain of prior contract, which gave outsider exclusive right to take at par shares of corporate stock to be thereafter issued.—Kingston v. Home Life Ins. Co. of America, 101 A. 898.

14-19. Though complainants acquired corporate stock without knowledge that corporation had previously given third person exclusive right to subscribe to corporate stock to be thereafter issued, that fact does not authorize complainants to attack contract.—Kingston v. Home Life Ins. Co. of America, 101 A. 898.

14-20 (Del. Ch. 1911.) Statements by one selling corporate stock that the investor was absolutely secure as to a certain amount per share, and that it was impossible for him to lose $5,000 on a purchase of 23 shares at a par value of $50, was not a statement of a material existing fact upon which the purchaser could rely to rescind the purchase for misrepresentations, being mere puffing as to future prospects.—Grone v. Economic Life Ins. Co., 80 A. 809.

14-21. A statement to a prospective purchaser of stock that the investment was absolutely secured for $10 a share by the law under which the corporation was incorporated was a representation as to the law, charging the purchaser with notice of the charter of the corporation and laws controlling it, so that he could not rely thereon as a misrepresentation in order to rescind the contract.—Grone v. Economic Life Ins. Co., 80 A. 809.

14-22. Since a statement to a purchaser of corporate stock that it was secured absolutely for $10 a share by the law under which the company was incorporated gave him notice of the source of the seller's statement, so that the purchaser had an equal opportunity with the seller to verify the statement, by referring to the law of incorporation, even though it were that of another state, and he could not rely thereon as a misrepresentation in order to rescind the contract, being bound to investigate for himself.—Grone v. Economic Life Ins. Co., 80 A. 809.

14-23. One who subscribed to corporate stock in reliance on the sound judgment and good faith of an old friend, who sold it to him, and not upon any statement of an existing fact made as to the character of the investment, could not rescind the contract for misrepresentations, though it proved to be a poor investment.—Grone v. Economic Life Ins. Co., 80 A. 809.

14-24. (Del. Ch. 1911.) Under a stock subscription at a premium above the par value of the stock, which provided that the subscriber took a certain number of shares, paying part cash and agreeing to pay the remainder in installments, payable without further notice thereafter until the full amount due was paid, whereupon a full-paid nonassessable certificate should be issued, the subscriber was not entitled to receive a certificate until he had paid both the par value of the stock and the premiums.—Grone v. Economic Life Ins., 80 A. 809.

See also Nos. 17-2, 17-12, 17-22, 23-8, 23-11, 24-10.

14c. Ultra Vires and Improperly Issued Stock.

14-25. (Del. Ch. 1911.) Stock subscriptions were not ultra vires, because made at a premium above the par value of the stock.—Grone v. Economic Life Ins. Co., 80 A. 809.

14-26. (Del. Ch.) An issue of common stock by a corporation to an associated corporation composed of organizers, men controlling first corporation, in consideration of a valueless business idea, is fraudulent and void.—Scully v. Automobile Finance Co., 101 A. 908.

14-27. (Del. Ch.) New shares of corporate stock cannot be issued for improper purpose, as to maintain control of corporation.—Kingston v. Home Life Ins. Co. of America, 101 A. 898.

14-28. Const. art. 9, s. 3., provides that no corporation shall issue stock, except for money paid, labor done, or personal property, or real estate or leases thereof. General Corporation Law, s. 14, provides that subscriptions to or purchases of the capital stock of any corporation may be paid for by cash, by labor done, by personal property, or by real property, or by leases thereof, and that, in the absence of fraud, the judgment of the directors as to the value of such labor, etc., shall be conclusive. Stock in a corporation was issued for property which was never delivered to the corporation, and the issue was ratified by the directors. Held, that such issue was unlawful and ultra vires, and might be questioned by other stockholders; it being a fraud upon the state, if upon no one else.—Ellis v. Penn Beef Co., 80 A. 666.

14-29. Where corporation had power to issue preferred stock, but exercised such power ineffectually or informally, stockholders taking stock are, as against creditors, estopped from urging invalidity of issue to escape payment.—John W. Cooney Co. v. Arlington Hotel Co., 101 A. 879.

14-30. (Del. Ch. 1911.) A stockholder of a corporation may sue in equity for the cancellation of an unlawful and ultra vires issue of stock, even though the stockholder, when he acquired his interest, had knowledge of that fact.—Ellis v. Penn Beef Co., 80 A. 666.

See also Nos. 6-29, 10-4, 17-4, 17-5, 17-7, 17-13, 17-20.

14d. Transfer of Stock.

14-31. Del. Laws, c. 147, s. 18, held not to render invalid an unrecorded transfer of a stockholder's shares as collateral security, as against attaching creditors.—Allen v. Stewart (Del. Ch.) 44 A. 786.

14-32. (Del. Ch.) Assignment in blank of certificate of stock, and delivery to purchaser, impliedly authorizes buyer to fill in name as assignee and transfer shares on company's books.—Lippman v. Kehoe Stenograph Co., 98 A. 943.

14-33. A by-law made by the directors of a bank that no stockholder should have the right to transfer his stock while he was a debtor to the bank, gives the bank a lien on the stock for the debts of the holder and is valid.—McDowell v. Bank of W. & B., 1 Harr. 27 (31, 32).

See also Nos. 6-1, 6-3, 6-11, 6-12, 8-3, 19-3.

14e. Unpaid Stock, Stockholders' Liability.

14-34. (Del. Ch.) Those acquiring corporate stock without formal subscription take it subject to statutory liability to make payment in full if necessary for benefit of creditors.—John W. Cooney Co. v. Arlington Hotel Co., 101 A. 879.

14-35. As to creditors, there is no difference between liability of holders of stock and subscribers to stock to pay par value of shares if necessary for payment of corporate debts.—John W. Cooney Co., v. Arlington Hotel Co., 101 A. 879.

14-36. (Del. Ch.) General Corporation Law, Sec. 13, declaring that holder of preferred stock shall not be personally liable for debts of corporation, does not exempt holders of preferred stock from calls or assessments up to par value for creditors, but merely exempts them from liability beyond that imposed by section 20.— John W. Cooney Co. v. Arlington Hotel Co., 101 A. 879.

14-37. (Del. Ch.) Holders of voting trust certificates to whom common stock was given as bonus on purchase of preferred stock held beneficial owners and liable to corporate creditors for amounts unpaid on common stock.—John W. Cooney Co. v. Arlington Hotel Co., 101 A. 879.

14-38. Persons who received common stock as bonus, voting trust certificates being issued, and stock having been delivered to trustee under such certificates, held bound for protection of corporate creditors to make payment of amount unpaid on their shares.— John W. Cooney Co. v. Arlington Hotel Co., 101 A. 879.

14-39. Though creditors of corporation knew at time of extending credit that its common stock was issued as bonus, holders of such common stock may be required to pay par value thereof for benefit of such creditors.—John W. Cooney Co. v. Arlington Hotel Co., 101 A. 879.

14-40. (Del. Ch.) Corporate stock issued and outstanding and not paid for is fund for benefit of creditors, and in general all who hold stock not paid for are liable to creditors for amount so unpaid. —John W. Cooney Co. v. Arlington Hotel Co., 101 A. 879.

14-41. (Del. Ch.) Delaware corporation cannot make subscription contract which will free subscriber from liability to pay for shares imposed by Delaware Incorporation Act, on stockholders for benefit of creditors.—John W. Cooney Co. v. Arlington Hotel Co., 101 A. 879.

14-42. Under General Corporation Law, Sec. 13, issue of preferred stock held not open to attack so as to enable subscribers to escape liability for unpaid subscriptions on ground that preferred stock amounted to more than two-thirds of capital of corporation.— Cooney v. Hotel Co., 101 A. 879.

14-43. (Del. Ch.) Creditors of corporation, where amounts due from shareholders on unpaid shares exceed amount of claims, are entitled to have interest calculated on their claims.—John W. Cooney Co. v. Arlington Hotel Co., 101 A. 879.

14-44. (Del. Ch.) Under General Corporation Law, s. 20-22, 49, 51, court of equity, a corporation having been adjudged insolvent and receivers appointed, has jurisdiction to estimate claims and assess stockholders who had not paid for their shares, or whose subscriptions were unpaid.—John W. Cooney Co. v. Arlington Hotel Co., 101 A. 879.

14-45. That corporation itself made call on stockholders to pay amounts due on shares subscribed for does not, after insolvency, prevent court from making call or assessment for protection of creditors.—John W. Cooney Co. v. Arlington Hotel Co., 101 A. 879.

14-46. Where corporate receiver had been appointed and assessment against stockholders who had not fully paid for their shares was necessary, such assessment should not be levied against stockholder who had been adjudicated bankrupt, but in absence of evidence no stockholders will be excluded on ground of financial irresponsibility.—John W. Cooney Co. v. Arlington Hotel Co., 101 A. 879.

14-47. (Del.) Although the General Corporation Law (22 Del. Laws, c. 394) provides that at no time shall the total of the preferred stock exceed two-thirds of the actual capital paid in cash or property, it is no defense to liability for unpaid preferred stock that the issue of preferred stock was void and not assessable for the debts of the company, because the common stock was not paid for in cash, since creditors may assume that the par value of common stock has been paid, so that the words of the statute, "actual capital paid in cash or property," mean, as to creditors, the par value of the common stock issued.—Du Pont v. Ball, 106 A. 39. Note: Act no longer requires preferred stock to exceed two-thirds of the common stock.

14-48. (Del.) Stockholder's liability for unpaid stock is unaffected by fact that corporation issued stock as full-paid and agreed that it should be nonassessable; such agreement being ultra vires and void, and the acceptance of stock raising an implied promise to pay therefor.—Du Pont v. Ball, 106 A. 39.

14-49. It is no defense to liability for unpaid stock that, the stock having been issued without consideration, contrary to the constitutional provision, the issue was ultra vires and void; the ultra vires feature of the transaction being, not the issuance, but the failure to exact payment for the stock, and the agreement that it need not be paid for.—Du Pont v. Ball, 106 A. 39.

See also No. 17-8.

14f. Capital, Capital Stock.

14-50. The word "capital," as used in the Delaware corporation law, prohibiting the use of corporate funds to purchase the corporation's own stock when it would impair the capital, prohibited such use when the value of the corporation's assets was less than the aggregate amount of all the shares of its capital stock.—In re International Radiator Co., 92 A. 355.

14-51. (Del.) The word "capital" does not mean the corpus of the property or the stock, but with reference to new stock, issued as stock dividend, is property or corpus; the property of the corporation being its real capital.—Bryan v. Aiken, 86 A. 674, 45 L. R. A. (N. S.) 477, reversing decree (Ch.) Same v. Aikin, 82 A. 817.

See also Nos. 15-1, 15-5, 17-3, 23-2, 23-9.

15. DIVIDENDS

15-1. (Del. Ch.) Distribution of shares of another company received by corporation in exchange for its mining property held illegal under General Incorporation Act, Sec. 35, forbidding any corporation from diminishing its capital stock.—Butler v. New Keystone Copper Co., 93 A. 380.

15-2. (Del.) Though net earnings of a corporation may be retained by it and invested for a period of years, yet when subsequently divided, by declaring a dividend in cash, stock, or both, it will be regarded as a distribution of profits.—Bryan v. Aiken, 86 A. 674, 45 L. R. A. (N. S.) 477, reversing decree (Ch.) Same v. Aikin, 82 A. 817.

15-3. As between the corporation and the stockholders, a stock dividend is a part of the capital.—(Ch.) Bryan v. Aikin, 82 A. 817, decree reversed (Sup.) Bryan v. Aiken, 86 A. 674, 45 L. R. A. (N. S.) 477.

15-4. (Del. Ch.) Dividends, which can be declared only out of surplus or profit arising from business, cannot be declared out of saving effected by corporate officer, or out of estimated enhancement in value of land purchased with corporate capital.—Kingston v. Home Life Ins. Co. of America, 101 A. 898.

15-5. (Del.) A corporation cannot decrease its capital stock by distributing it among the stockholders as dividends.—(Ch.) Bryan

v. Aikin, 82 A. 817, decree reversed (Sup.) Bryan v. Aiken, 86 A. 674, 45 L. R. A. (N. S.) 477.

See also Nos. 17-6, 20-1, 23-9, 31-48.

16. INCORPORATORS

No decisions.

See also No. 6-33.

17. STOCKHOLDERS

17a. Relation of Stockholders to Corporation.

17-1. Under stock subscriptions, subscribers assume the relation of stockholders, and not creditors, with reference to assets on dissolution.—Grone v. Economic Life Ins. Co., 80 A. 809.

17-2. (Del. Ch.) The fact that one person owns all the stock in a corporation does not merge his identity with that of the corporation.—Martin v. D. B. Martin Co., 88 A .612.

See also No. 31-63.

17b. Powers and Rights of Stockholders.

17-3. (Del.) Where a contract between a private corporation and an insurance company whereby the corporation has a perpetual and exclusive option to purchase the stock of the insurance company, operates prejudicially to the minority stockholders of the insurance company, they may bring a bill to have such contract terminated.—Kingston v. Home Life Ins. Co. of America, 104 A. 25, affirming decree (Ch) 101 A. 898.

17-4. (Del. Ch.) Preferred stockholders may bring suit to cancel common stock illegally issued in consideration of a valueless business idea.—Scully v. Automobile Finance Co., 101 A. 908.

17-5. Where it is certain that a corporation will not act, the stockholder need not apply to the corporation before suing to cancel stock unlawfully issued.—Ellis v. Penn Beef Co., 80 A. 666.

17-6. (Del. Super. 1908.) A shareholder in a corporation has no property interest in the profits of the business carried on by the corporation until a dividend has been declared out of such profits.—Pyle v. Gallaher, 75 A. 373, 6 Pennewill, 407.

17-7. Preferred stockholders have a right to question legality of issue of common stock.—Scully v. Automobile Finance Co., 101 A. 908.

17-8. (Del.) That a creditor actually participated in the issuance of unpaid stock as full-paid and nonassessable, or consented thereto, does not estop him from enforcing, a: a statutory liability on unpaid stock, his claim against other stockholders, to whom such stock was issued with his assistance or acquiescence, where there was no intention on his part to perpetrate a fraud upon the others, or gain an

61

unfair advantage by the transaction.—Du Pont v. Ball 106 A. 39.

17-9. (Del.) Stockholders should not be assessed, and required to pay their assessments, before their legal liability is definitely determined, because the amounts assessed may be much in excess of what they are legally liable to pay.—Du Pont v. Ball, 106 A. 39.

17-10. A stockholder has a right to inspect and make extracts from the corporation's books at a proper time and for proper purposes.—State v. Jessup & Moore Paper Co., 77 A. 16.

17-11. A holder of one-twentieth of the stock of a corporation, which has no market value, which he was forced to acquire to protect himself, and which he desires to sell, is entitled to inspect, and make extracts of, the corporate books, to ascertain its value; the corporation having refused to give him the information.—State v. Jessup & Moore Paper Co., 77 A. 16.

17-12. (Del. Ch.) Shareholders' pre-emptive right to subscribe to shares of corporate stock in preference to outsiders is well established.—Kingston v. Home Life Ins. Co. of America, 101 A. 898.

17c. **Duties and Liabilities of Stockholders.**

See also Nos. 6-13, 6-23, 6-25, 8-1, 8-10, 14-1, 14-2, 14-4, 14-11, 14-28, 14-43, 15-3, 23-9, 23-10, 28-8, 31-25, 31-30, 31-31, 31-46.

17-13. Purchasers of preferred stock who received voting trust certificates for common stock issued as bonus held chargeable with that knowledge, and not entitled to attack validity of preferred stock issue on ground that there had been no compliance with General Corporation Law Sec. 13.—John W. Cooney Co. v. Arlington Hotel Co., 101 A. 879.

17-14. (Del. Ch.) Contingent liability of stockholders for debts of corporation in amount to which they are indebted for their shares is equitable asset which vests in receivers, or at least is enforceable by such receivers for benefit of all creditors who come in the case.—John W. Cooney Co. v. Arlington Hotel Co., 101 A. 879.

17-15. (Del. Ch.) Stockholders liable to assessment for amounts unpaid on their shares who are also creditors cannot set off amount which they will be assessed against debts due them, but must pay their assessment and share in fund when realized.—John W. Cooney Co. v. Arlington Hotel Co., 101 A. 879.

17-16. A person may waive the provisions of statutes made for his particular and personal protection, and which he may waive without infringing on the rights of others or affecting public policy; but one may not waive a constitutional or statutory provision fixing the voting power of stock in corporations.—Brooks v. State, 79 A. 790.

17-17. Where necessary for protection of creditors, etc., held that corporate receivers might collect entire sum necessary to defray obligations, etc., from responsible stockholder who owed such amount on his unpaid shares.—John W. Cooney Co. v. Arlington Hotel Co., 101 A. 879.

17-18. Stockholder's liability in addition to unpaid subscriptions, as under a "double liability" statute, is not resorted to if the assets of the corporation, including unpaid subscriptions, are sufficient to pay creditors.—Du Pont v. Ball, 106 A. 39.

17-19. The liability of stockholders for unpaid subscriptions is unaffected by creditors' knowledge or lack of knowledge of the facts and circumstances under which the stock was issued.—Du Pont v. Ball, 106 A. 39.

17-20. One subscribing for and accepting preferred stock for his own benefit, and holding himself as the legal owner thereof, is estopped to deny liability as stockholder to bona fide creditors on the ground that his stock was illegally issued and void.—Du Pont v. Ball, 106 A. 39.

17-21. As to stockholders' liability for unpaid stock, there is no distinction or priority of liability between stock subscribed for and that which is issued and accepted without being paid for, or between preferred and common stock; the test under the statute being not the class or character of the stock, but whether it has been paid for. —Du Pont v. Ball, 106 A. 39.

17-22. A subscriber may be sued for arrears of subscription for stock due from him without proof that certificates of stock have been issued or tendered to him by the company.—Del. R. R. Co. v. Tharp, 1 Houst. 149 (174 et seq).

See also Nos. 8-6, 8-9, 10-7, 10-24, 10-28, 14-5, 14-16, 14-42, 14-44, 14-45, 14-46, 14-48, 24-10, 31-55, 31-56, 31-59, 31-60, 31-61, 31-62, 31-65.

18. VOTING TRUSTS, TRUSTEES AND PROXIES

No decisions.
See also Nos. 14-37, 14-38, 19-8, 19-10.

19. DIRECTORS

19a. Qualification of Directors.

19-1. Person maintaining home in Pennsylvania, for self and wife, habitually sleeping and taking part of meals there, who had been officially denied right of citizenship in Delaware, held not a resident within General Corporation Act, s. 9, requiring that one director be such.—Lippman v. Kehoe Stenograph Co., 98 A. 943.

Note: Law requiring residence of one director no longer in effect.

19-2. (Del. Ch.) Fact that not one of directors of corporation was resident, as required by General Corporation Act, s. 9, requiring one resident member, did not invalidate their election or affect validity of their acts as a board.—Lippman v. Kehoe Stenograph Co., 98 A. 943.

Note: Law requiring residence of one director no longer in effect.

19-3. Where director at request of one acting for corporation assigned his stock certificate in blank, but no transfer was entered on corporate books, and it was not contemplated either by director or company that he had lost his status as stockholder so as to be ineligible, such director was still eligible to act in that capacity.—Lippman v. Kehoe Stenograph Co., 102 A. 988.

See also Nos. 6-2, 6-3, 6-4, 6-16, 6-17, 6-21, 6-26.

19b. Powers and Duties of Directors.

19-4. (Del. Ch.) Judgment of directors of corporation as to wisdom of exchanging its property for stock in another company, if legal, held not subject to judicial review.—Butler v. New Keystone Copper Co., 93 A. 380.

19-5. (Del. Ch.) Notwithstanding the distinct legal entities of two corporations, persons who are directors and agents in each of two corporations cannot represent both in a transaction in which the interests of the two are opposed.—Martin v. D. R. Martin Co., 88 A. 612.

19-6. (Del. Ch. 1911.) Where the directors of a corporation engaged in selling its lots informed the purchasers that the space between the ocean and a certain street should be open, the authority of the directors to make such declarations cannot be questioned in a proceeding to secure a preliminary injunction to restrain the obstruction of such space.—Poole v. Commissioners of Rehoboth, 80 A. 683.

19-7. (Del. Super. 1911.) That, without official action, a majority of the directors of a corporation orally authorized plaintiff's officer to sell a machine, owned by the corporation, and to sue for the price, is insufficient to show plaintiff's right to recover the price —Mattoax Leather Co. v Patzowsky, 80 A 241

See also Nos 6-18, 10-8, 13-3, 14-28, 31-22, 31-35, 31-69

19c. Rights of Directors.

19-8. (Del. Ch.) A director of a corporation is an "officer," within General Corporation Act, Sec. 57, and is not entitled to priority for wages—In re Peninsula Cut Stone Co., 82 A. 689, 9 Del. Ch. 348.

19d. Meetings of Directors.

19-9. (Del. Ch.) Corporate directors can act as a board, not as individuals, but only at a board meeting.—U. S. Fire Apparatus Co. v. G. W. Baker Mach. Co., 95 A. 294.

19-10. Directors must be personally present at board meetings, and cannot vote by proxy.—Lippman v. Kehoe Stenograph Co., 95 A. 895.

19-11. Though a director of a corporation was bound by a waiver of notice of a directors' meeting signed by him after the meeting, another director was not bound by such waiver.—Lippman v. Kehoe Stenograph Co., 95 A. 895.

19-12. Director signing notice of meeting held not to agree that another director should discharge duty or make quorum by signing minutes subsequent to meeting.—Lippman v. Kehoe Stenograph Co., 95 A. 895.

19-13. General Corporation Law, Sec. 138 (Railroad), does not authorize a director to waive notice of a special meeting of the directors after the meeting.—Lippman v. Kehoe Stenograph Co., 95 A. 895.

See also Nos. 6-15, 6-19, 6-20, 6-22, 6-23, 6-24, 6-25, 6-27.

20. OFFICERS

20-1. (Del. Ch.) Statutory liability of officers who improperly declare dividend cannot be enforced in action against corporation and another company to annul contracts, enjoin payments of dividends, etc., officers not being parties.—Kingston v. Home Life Ins. Co. of America, 101 A. 898.

20-2. On a contract made with a corporate officer such officer may bring a suit in his own name for enforcement.—Norton v. Janvier, 5 Harr. 346 (347).

See also Nos. 6-6, 7-2, 8-11, 10-18, 24-7, 25-2, 28-6, 31-21, 31-23, 31-35.

21. AGENTS
No decisions.
See Nos. 8-11, 10-11.

22. EMPLOYEES
No decisions.

23. CORPORATE POWERS

23-1. (Del. Ch. 1898.) Where the charter of complainant's grantor, a private corporation, had become void before it took title to the property in question by reason of its failure to record its charter within the time limited by the general statute, but such charter was duly recorded in accordance with 13 Del. Laws 1869, p. 356, c. 389, extending the time for recording private acts, and providing that acts so recorded should have the same force and effect as if recorded according to law, and complainant's charter was renewed 21 days after its expiration by 17 Del. Laws 1885, p. 974, c. 720, the corporation being continued 20 years from the passage of the renewing act, complainant and its grantor had sufficient corporate capacity to convey a good title to the land in question.—Diamond State Iron Co. v. Husbands, 68 A. 240, 8 Del. Ch. 205.

23-2. (Del. Ch.) A corporation may pledge its unissued shares as collateral for a loan made to it, and when stock is so pledged the creditor may prove his debt against the corporation's receiver and return the stock.—In re International Radiator Co., 92 A. 255.

23-3. (Del. Ch.) A clause in a mortgage given by a public service corporation that it shall include after-acquired property is valid.— In re Frederica Water, Light & Power Co., 93 A. 376

23-4. (Del. Ch.) 20 Del. Laws, c. 579, amending the chattel mortgage law, held intended to validate the lien of mortgages, upon both real and personal property.—National Bank of Wilmington & Brandywine v. Wilmington, N. C. & S. Ry. Co., 81 A. 70, 9 Del. Ch. 258.

23-5. (Del. Ch.) Holders of corporate bonds secured by mortgage covering after-acquired property take the after-acquired property subject to any existing liens.—In re Frederica Water Light & Power Co., 93 A. 376.

23-6. (Del. 1904.) General Corporation Law 1901, s. 3, (22 Del. Laws, p. 287, c. 167), providing that, in addition to the powers enumerated in section 2 of the act, "every corporation" shall possess and exercise all the powers and privileges contained in the act and the powers expressly given in its charter or certificate under which it was incorporated, so far as the same are necessary or convenient to the attainment of the objects set forth in such charter or certificate, subject to the provisions of the act corporations created prior to the Constitution in force at the time of the passage of the act, as well as those created after the promulgation thereof.—Bay State Gas Co. v. State, 56 A. 1114, 4 Pennewill, 238.

23-7. (Del. Sup.) That 26 Del. Laws, c. 189, grants to boulevard corporations franchises ordinarily exercised by separate and distinct corporations, does not render it invalid.—Clendaniel v. Conrad, 83 A. 1036, 3 Boyce, 549, Ann. Cas. 1913 B. 968.

23-8. (Del. Ch.) Ordinarily a corporation may purchase its own stock, when the purchase does not diminish its ability to pay debts or lessen the security of its creditors.—In re International Radiator Co., 92 A. 255.

23-9. (Del.) A corporation has power either to distribute the corporate earnings to stockholders or to withhold them, and may increase the capital stock by stock dividends.—(Ch.) Bryan v. Aikin, 82 A. 817, decree reversed (Sup.) Bryan v. Aiken, 86 A. 674, 45 L. R. A. (N. S.) 477.

23-10. (Del. Ch.) If business of a corporation is unprofitable or hopeless holders of majority of stock may, against dissent of minority, sell all its property to wind up its affairs.—Butler v. New Keystone Copper Co., 93 A. 380.

23-11. (Del. Ch.) Under General Incorporation Act, Sec. 3, and s. 5, par. 8, and provisions of its charter, held, that mining company might in good faith and for an adequate consideration exchange its mining property for shares of another mining company.—Butler v. New Keystone Copper Co., 93 A. 380.

23-12. In replevin for a sewing machine leased by a corporation, the defendant was estopped from denying the authority of the plaintiff to transact the business; she having contracted with it.— Standard Sewing-Mach. Co. v. Frame. (Del. Super.) 48 A. 188.

23-13. A corporation cannot deny its existence in order to escape liability on a contract entered into by it when in the apparent exercise of its corporate franchises and powers.—Brady v. Delaware Mut. Life Ins. Co. (Del. Super.) 45 A. 345.

23-14. A provision in the charter of a company that in order to enable the managers to pay the debts already contracted by them, or which may hereafter be contracted, or to reimburse to them any money which they, or either of them, shall advance in payment of such debts, or otherwise, for the use of the company, they shall have a claim and lien upon the proceeds of the sale of property of the company etc.; held, to give a legal remedy against the company.— Stephens v. Green H. Cem. Co., 1 Houst. 26 (29 et seq).

23-15. The right of the Legislature to bestow on corporations the power of internal regulation, and the capacity of corporations to receive and exercise such power, even though it involve legislative power within the corporate limits, exist at common law, and are recognized by the Constitution. (Art. 2, s. 17; Art 7, s. 8).—Rice v. Foster, 4 Harr, 479 (503).

23-16. A corporation cannot, in general, make any contract which is not necessary, directly or incidentally, for the objects of its corporation; but it may make any contract, either as principal or surety, proper for the usual and ordinary means of carrying on its business.—Derringer's Admr. v. Derringer's Admr. 5 Houst. 416 (428).

23-17. A gas light company is a corporation "for public improvement" within Const. 1831, art. 2, s. 17.—City of Wilmington v. Addicks (Del. Ch.) 43 A. 297.

23-18. Statements of a loan association issued in lieu of certificates under the corporate seal, though not authorized by the company's charter or by-laws, are valid, where they are recognized by the company in the ordinary course of business.—Richardson v. Delaware Loan Ass'n. (Del. Super.) 32 A. 980.

See also Nos. 14-29, 14-50, 19-5, 19-6, 24-8, 30-2, 37-6.

24. CORPORATE RIGHTS

24-1. Const. 1831, art. 2, s. 17, and Const. 1897, art. 9, s. 1, held not to prohibit the legislature from enacting general incorporation laws which will revoke exclusive privileges held by a corporation organized prior to 1897.—Wilmington City Ry. Co. v. People's Ry. Co. (Del. Ch.) 47 A. 245.

24-2. Under Const. 1831, art. 2, s. 17, the legislature may withdraw one or more of the privileges granted to a corporation without revoking the entire charter.—City of Wilmington v. Addicks. (Del. Ch.) 47 A. 366.

24-3. The revocation contemplated by Const. 1831, art. 2, s. 17, may be either direct or by necessary implication, by the passage of an act necessarily inconsistent with some right or privilege possessed by an existing corporation.—Wilmington City Ry. Co. v. Wilmington & B. S. Ry. Co. (Del. Ch.) 46 A. 12.

24-4. The provision in Const. 1831, art. 2, s. 17, permits the withdrawal of a single right or privilege, without revoking the whole franchise.—Wilmington City Ry. Co. v. Wilmington & B. S. Ry. Co. (Del. Ch.) 46 A. 12.

24-5. A corporation cannot be summoned as a garnishee.—Holland v. Leslie, 2 Harr. 306 (307).

24-6. The right of a corporation de facto to exist can be inquired into only by quo warranto in the name of the state.—City of Wilmington v. Addicks (Del. Ch.) 43 A. 297.

24-7. (Del. Super. 1909.) In trover for certificates of stock alleged to have been converted by the corporation, it is a defense to show that an officer of the corporation converted them individually.—Layman v. F. F. Slocomb & Co., 76 A. 1094, 7 Pennewill, 403.

24-8. (Del.) By comity a corporation created by one sovereignty is permitted to make contracts in another and sue thereon.—Model Heating Co. v. Magarity, 81 A. 394, 2 Boyce, 459, L. R. A. 1915 B. 665.

24-9. Corporations are collections of individuals entitled to the same protection to property in their aggregate or corporate capacity as are individuals.—Smyrna, etc., S. S. Co. v. Whilldin, 4 Harr. 228 (230).

24-10. Independent of statute, unpaid capital due from stock holders is part of assets of corporation, and so belongs to it and not to creditors.—John W. Cooney Co. v. Arlington Hotel Co., 101 A. 879.

24-11. The police power of the State comprehends all those general powers of internal regulation necessary to secure the peace, good order, health, welfare and comfort of society; but it would seem that it cannot, under color of such law, destroy or impair the franchise itself, nor any of those rights and powers which are essential to its beneficial exercise, such as restricting the right of a railroad to adjust its tariff of charges.—P. W. & B. R. R. Co. v. Bowers, 4 Houst. 506 (536 et seq.)

24-12. Charters of corporations, excepting only those which are strictly civil or municipal, are within the clause of the U. S. Constitution which declares that no State shall pass any "law impairing the obligation of contracts," and any Legislative act which abridges any power or privilege vested by the charter, which is material to the exercise of the franchise granted, unless the right to pass such an act be usual, and without the consent of the corporation, is invalid as impairing the obligation of contracts.—P. W. B. R. R. Co. v. Bowers, 4 Houst. 506 (528 et seq); Rice v. Foster, 4 Harr. i479 (491,492); Bailey v. P. W. & B. R. R. Co., 4 Harr. 389 (399 et seq).

24-13. Legislative restrictions on the passage of any law impairing vested rights, or altering the charter of a corporation is considered at length in Bailey v. P. W. & B. R. R. Co., 4 Harr. 489.

See also 30-1.

25. CORPORATE DUTIES

25-1. (Del. Ch. 1910.) The grant to a corporation organized to operate as a private business enterprise, works of general public utility under grants of a franchise or a monopoly, or of the right of eminent domain, is subject to an implied condition that the corporation will assume an obligation to fulfill the purposes on account of which the grant was made.—Thoroughgood v. Georgetown Water Co., 77 A. 720.

25-2. (Del. 1910.) A domestic corporation cannot excuse nonperformance of duty by showing that the duty rested primarily on nonresident officers.—State v. Jessup & Moore Paper Co., 77 A. 16.

25-3. (Del. Super. 1902.) A corporation cannot defeat recovery for money borrowed which it actually received and enjoyed, though it was not borrowed, or the note therefor executed, as provided by its by-laws.—St. Joseph's Polish Catholic Beneficial Soc. v. St. Hedwig's Church, 53 A. 353, 4 Pennewill, 141.

25-4. A corporation is liable for its servants' negligence.—Wilson v. Rockland Mfg. Co., 2 Harr. 67 (70).

26. CORPORATE DISABILITIES AND LIMITATIONS
No decisions.

27. PERIOD OF EXISTENCE

27-1. A corporation becomes absolutely dissolved upon the ex-

piration of the period of its charter, not merely dormant.—Com.
Bank v. Lockwood's Admr., 4 Harr. 8 (11 et seq).

28. TERMINATION OF CORPORATE FRANCHISE

28-1. (Del. Ch.) The power of a chancery court, under General
Corporation Act, Sec. 43, to appoint a receiver for a dissolved corporation, is not limited to three years from dissolution, notwithstanding
section 40.—Slaughter v. Moore, 82 A. 963; 9 Del. Ch. 350.

28-2. Where the grantor of land conveyed to a corporation has
received a valuable consideration therefor, on the dissolution of the
corporation, a trust will be declared in favor of stockholders or
creditors, and the grantor may be compelled to convey the legal
title to such persons beneficially interested.—Diamond State Iron
Co. v. Husbands, 68 A. 240, 8 Del. Ch. 205.

28-3. (Del. Ch. 1911.) A corporation which for two years has
failed to pay its franchise tax, so that its charter and powers have,
under Franchise Tax Act (21 Del. Laws, c. 166) s. 10, become inoper-
ative and void, and whose charter the Governor has proclaimed repealed, as required by section 11, is within General Corporation
Act (22 Del. Laws, c. 166) s. 43, providing that "when a corporation
* * * shall be dissolved in any manner whatever" a court of chancery
may appoint a receiver for it.—Harned v. Beacon Hill Real Estate
Co., 80 A. 805.

28-4. The power given a court of chancery by General Corporation Act (22 Del. Laws, c. 166) s. 43, to appoint a receiver for a
dissolved corporation "at any time," is not limited to the three
years from expiration or dissolution of a corporation, for which section 40 provides its corporate existence shall be continued for winding up its affairs.—Harned v. Beacon Hill Real Estate Co., 80 A.
805.

28-5. Though the three years after dissolution of a corporation, for which its corporate existence is extended by General Corporation Act (22 Del. Laws, c. 166) s. 40, for winding up its affairs,
has expired, the power given a court of chancery by section 43, at
any time, on application of a creditor or stockholder of a dissolved
corporation, to appoint a receiver for the final settlement of its unfinished business, may be exercised on an application in the nature
of a bill against the corporation, to which its officers may answer.—
Harned v. Beacon Hill Real Estate Co., 80 A. 805.

28-6. Evidence in proceedings to liquidate the assets of a corporation after dissolution held to show that an officer "advanced" money
to the corporation as a loan and not as a gift.—Grone v. Economic
Life Ins. Co., 80 A. 809.

28-7. (Del. Ch. 1911.) In analogy to the equitable principles governing the action of assumpsit, one who advanced money to a corporation to carry on its business is entitled to recover such advances in a proceeding to liquidate the assets on dissolution.—Grone v. Economic Life Ins. Co., 80 A. 809.

28-8. Where stock subscriptions provided no time for the payment of installments due, and no default in payments on demand made is shown, all subscribers should receive a proportionate share of the corporate assets on dissolution, irrespective of whether their payments on the installments have been equal in amounts or paid at the same time.—Grone v. Economic Life Ins. Co., 80 A. 809.

28-9. (Del. Ch. 1898.) The rule that on dissolution of a corporation title to its real estate reverts to the grantor, or his heirs, is applicable to the legal title only, and is subject to the equitable principle that such reversioner would take title in trust for him who possessed the beneficial interest by reason of having paid a valuable consideration for the land.—Diamond State Iron Co. v. Husbands, 68 A. 240, 8 Del. Ch. 205.

28-10. Even if, under General Corporation Act (22 Del. Laws, c. 166), s. 43, authorizing a court of chancery, on application of a creditor or stockholder of a dissolved corporation, to continue its directors as trustees, or appoint a receiver for final settlement of its unfinished business, reason for appointing a receiver, rather than continuing the directors as trustees, should be shown, it is enough that nothing remains to be administered but a form, which the corporation attempted to sell and convey unsuccessfully, because more than three years after its dissolution, that complainant is interested personally, as well as a stockholder, to have good title made, that all management of the corporation's affairs has long been abandoned by its officers, and that its president and two of its directors have signed an answer consenting to appointment of a receiver to displace them.—Harned v. Beacon Hill Real Estate Co., 80 A. 805.

See also Nos. 14-12, 17-1, 28-1, 30-3, 31-5, 31-6, 31-7.

29. FORFEITURE OF CORPORATE FRANCHISE AND REVOCATION OF CHARTER

29-1. (Del.) Under General Corporation Law, Sec. 43, held, that a corporation dissolved for nonpayment of franchise taxes is properly made a party defendant in a receivership action, unaffected by section 40.—Harned v. Beacon Hill Real Estate Co., 84 A. 229, 9, Del. Ch. 411, affirming decree (Ch.) 80 A. 805, 9 Del. Ch. 232.

29-2. The power of the Legislature to revoke corporate charters need not be expressed in the charter. It is reserved by the Constitution.—Del. R. R. Co. v. Tharp, 5 Harr. 454 (456).

29-3. The power of Legislature to revoke charters is not arbitrary, and may be exercised only upon cause.—S. C. 5 Harr. 454 (456).

29-4. A reservation, expressed in a charter, of the power of revocation "on conviction of misuse or abuse of privileges," is constitutional.—S. C. 5 Harr, 454 (456).

See also Nos. 28-1, 30-3.

30. VOLUNTARY DISSOLUTION

30-1. (Del. Ch.) Where a corporation ceases operation and is dissolved, its affairs being wound up by a receiver, latter may terminate executory contracts without increasing liability of estate by reason of further nonperformance.—Fell v. Securities Co. of North America, 97 A. 610.

30-2. (Del. Ch.) A distribution of all the assets of a company operating under the General Incorporation Act would be a winding up, which could be done legally only by the method provided by law.—Butler v. New Keystone Copper Co., 93 A. 380.

30-3. (Del. Ch. 1911.) The receipt of part repayment of money "advanced" to a corporation by its officer negatived a waiver by him of all right to repayment of the amount advanced, so that he could claim the remainder thereof in proceedings to liquidate the corporate assets on dissolution.—Grone v. Economic Life Ins. Co., 80 A. 809.

See also Nos. 10-5, 14-12, 17-1, 28-1, 28-2, 28-3, 28-4, 28-5, 28-6, 28-7, 28-10, 31-6.

31. INSOLVENCY

31a. Assignments for Benefit of Creditors.

31-1. The fact that an assignment by a corporation of its property in trust for creditors becoming parties thereto makes no provision for the return to the debtor of any surplus after the payment of such creditors does not prevent the assignment from being an assignment for the benefit of creditors, within Rev. Code 1852, amended to 1893, p. 960, c. 132, s. 4, making assignments in contemplation of insolvency void, where it was known to all the parties that there could not possibly be any surplus.—Brown v. Wilmington & Brandywine Leather Co., 74 A. 1105.

31-2. An assignment by a failing corporation of practically all of its property, in trust to sell the property and pay the proceeds ratably to such creditors as shall become parties thereto and accept their shares in full of their claims, is void, within Rev. Code 1852, amended to 1893, p. 960, c. 132, s. 4, making assignments for benefit

of certain creditors by a debtor in contemplation of insolvency void.
—Brown v. Wilmington & Brandywine Leather Co., 74 A. 1105.

31-3. Under Rev. Code 1852, amended to 1893, p. 960, c. 132, s. 4, providing that assignments in contemplation of insolvency for the benefit of preferred creditors shall be void, an assignment by a corporation in failing circumstances of its property for the benefit of certain creditors to the exclusion of the others is void.—Brown v. Wilmington & Brandywine Leather Co., 74 A. 1105.

31-4. An assignment by a failing manufacturing corporation of all its finished product, book accounts, and bills receivable, in trust to sell the assets and distribute the proceeds among such creditors as should become parties thereto and accept their shares in full of their claims, is not a sale, but is an assignment, within Rev. Code 1852, amended to 1893, p. 960, c. 132, s. 4, forbidding perpetual assignments for benefit of creditors, where, even if the agreement of the assenting creditors to accept their pro rata share in full of their claims, was a sufficient consideration for the property transferred, there was no such agreement in fact.—Brown v. Wilmington & Brandywine Leather Co., 74 A. 1105.

See also No. 30-1.

31b. Insolvency and Dissolution.

31-5. The appointment of a receiver for a corporation does not dissolve it, or terminate its legal existence.—Du Pont v. Standard Arms Co., 81 A. 1089, 9 Del. Ch. 315.

31-6. (Del. Ch.) Appointment of receivers and administration of an insolvent corporation's assets did not effect a dissolution.—Hirschfield v. Reading Finance & Securities Co., 82 A. 690, 9 Del. Ch. 344.

31-7. Deprivation of a corporation of its books and records on sale of its assets, by receivers, did not work a dissolution of the corporation.—Hirschfield v. Reading Finance & Securities Co., 82, A. 690, 9 Del. Ch. 344.

31-8. (Del. Ch.) Under an act authorizing appointment of a receiver for a corporation on ground of insolvency, held, that insolvency may consist of a deficiency of assets over liabilities, or inability to meet financial obligations as they mature in usual course, or both.—Whitmer v. William Whitmer & Sons, 99 A. 428.

31-9. (Del. Ch.) Where deficiency of assets is basis of a claim of insolvency, an affirmative showing that corporation has met all obligations and can continue to do so sufficiently established ability of corporation to meet its liabilities for purpose of a motion for a receiver pendente lite on that ground.—Whitmer v. William Whitmer & Sons, 99 A. 428.

See also Nos. 10-5, 14-44.

31c. Allegations of Insolvency and Appointment of Receivers.

31-10. (Del. Ch.) While the jurisdictional allegations of a bill for a receiver of a corporation on the ground of its insolvency consist of averments that the defendant is a corporation of the state, is insolvent, and is not a corporation for public improvement, still a bill which only contains such bald averments, though not perhaps demurrable, would not show grounds for the exercise of judicial discretion.—Sill v. Kentucky Coal & Timber Development Co., 97 A. 617.

31-11. (Del. Ch.) Under a statute authorizing appointment of a receiver for a corporation on ground of insolvency, if a receiver pendente lite is desired, facts to justify such relief should be stated, and a prayer therefor be included, in bill.—Whitmer v. William Whitmer & Sons, 99 A. 428.

31-12. (Del. Ch.) Where insolvency of a corporation is denied, and evidence is conflicting, a motion for receiver pendente lite on that ground should not be granted.—Whitmer v. William Whitmer & Sons, 99 A. 428.

31-13. Where a receiver pendente lite is sought for a corporation, whether or not insolvent, it is essential to show a reasonable apprehension of danger and an irreparable loss to subject-matter of suit before a final hearing can be had.—Whitmer v. Wm. Whitmer & Sons, 99 A. 428.

31-14. (Del. Ch.) Under a statute authorizing appointment of a receiver for a corporation on ground of insolvency, it is always discretionary whether such receiver be appointed.—Whitmer v. William Whitmer & Sons, 99 A. 428.

31-15. (Del. Ch.) Under a statute authorizing appointment of a receiver for a corporation on ground of insolvency if there be doubt as to proof of jurisdictional fact, insolvency court should not act.—Whitmer v. William Whitmer & Sons, 99 A. 428.

31-16. (Del. Ch.) Mismanagement of corporate affairs is not a necessary element of a bill for the appointment of a receiver for the corporation.—Sill v. Kentucky Coal & Timber Development Co., 97 A. 617.

31-17. (Del. Ch.) To entitle an interested party to the appointment of a receiver for an alleged insolvent corporation, it is not necessary that the complainant be a judgment creditor.—Sill v. Kentucky Coal & Timber Development Co., 97 A. 617.

31-18. (Del. Ch.) A bill for a receiver of a water company, alleging insolvency, that the margin of income for necessary repairs and improvements was more than absorbed by interest payable on bonds, that the plant was in great need of repairs, and that a failure to appoint a receiver would result in great loss, and would leave the city without adequate water supply, was sufficient to justify the appointment of a receiver with limited powers.—Thoroughgood v. Georgetown Water Co., 82 A. 689, 9 Del. Ch. 330.

31-19. (Del. Ch. 1910.) A corporation furnishing water to the inhabitants of a town, and to the town for municipal purposes, including service to fire plugs, and occupying the streets of the town with its conduits, though the corporation has not been given the right of eminent domain, or any other right usually accorded to quasi public corporations, is a "corporation for public improvement," within the statute providing that the act authorizing the appointment of a receiver of an insolvent corporation shall not apply to a corporation for public improvement.—Thoroughgood v. Georgetown Water Co., 77 A. 720.

31-20. (Del. Ch. 1910.) The statute authorizing the appointment of a receiver of an insolvent corporation on the application of a creditor is remedial, and gives to equity powers it did not previously possess; and it may appoint a receiver of a corporation solely on the ground of insolvency, on the application of a simple creditor, but the mere insolvency of a public service corporation does not justify the appointment of a receiver therefor.—Thoroughgood v. Georgetown Water Co., 77 A. 720.

31-21. Equity, independent of statutes, may appoint a receiver of a corporation, and through it take possession of its property and administer its affairs because of gross mismanagement, positive misconduct, or other breach of trust by its officers, and probably, except in rare cases, only when insolvency has resulted from such misconduct; the power of equity being within its power to grant relief to prevent injuries to property rights where no adequate relief is given at law.—Thoroughgood v. Georgetown Water Co., 77 A. 720.

31-22. That the majority of the directors of a public service corporation are nonresidents, and that they have removed the books of the corporation, do not justify the appointment of a receiver; for the nonresident officers may conduct the business of the corporation through others, and neither minority stockholders nor directors may disturb the control of the majority merely because they do not attend in person to the corporate affairs.—Thoroughgood v. Georgetown Water Co., 77 A. 720.

31-23. The fact that officers of a public service corporation are absent from the state, so that there is no one with authority to expend the income of the corporation for necessary repairs, without which the plant may deteriorate, to the loss of creditors and stockholders, does not justify the appointment of a receiver; the income of the corporation being largely in excess of the operating expenses, and those managing the affairs applying the income to the payment of interest on the bonds rather than in keeping up the plant, and it not appearing that the deterioration of the plant has reached such a stage as to jeopardize its efficiency.—Thoroughgood v. Georgetown Water Co., 77 A. 720.

31-24. (Del. Ch. 1911.) The mere fact that a corporation is new does not warrant an inference of its insolvency, on a question of the propriety of appointing a receiver.—Gray v. Council of Town of Newark, 79 A. 739.

31-25. (Del. Ch. 1910.) A stockholder of a public service corporation may not sue for the appointment of a receiver of the corporation on the ground of insolvency.—Thoroughgood v. Georgetown Water Co., 77 A. 720.

31-26. A bondholder of a public service corporation executing a mortgage to secure its bonds may not sue for the appointment of a receiver of the corporation, but he must enforce his rights through the trustee in the mortgage.—Thoroughgood v. Georgetown Water Co., 77 A. 720.

31-27. Under a statute authorizing appointment of a receiver for a corporation on the ground of insolvency, where evidence was conflicting as to fact of insolvency, and does not establish threatened loss or injury to creditors, or irregularities in management, held, that appointment of a receiver pendente lite will not be granted.— Shaw v. Standard Piano Co., 97 A. 281.

31-28. (Del. Ch. 1910.) A corporation made an assignment of its finished manufactured product, book accounts, and bills receivable, in trust to sell the assets and divide the proceeds ratably among such creditors as should become parties thereto and accept their shares in full of their claims. Prior to the execution of the assignment by the last creditor agreeing to it, the corporation and such creditors agreed that the corporation should transfer to the trustee the factory and machinery then owned by it to liquidate the claims of such creditors, unless the corporation should reorganize within a specified time. The appointment of a receiver prevented the favored creditors from obtaining the benefit of this agreement. The corporation was hopelessly insolvent, and knew it, and had no real intention of continuing business in its name or for any appreciable length of time. Held, that the assignment and agreement must be construed as constituting a single assignment, within Rev. Code 1852, amended to 1893, p. 960, c. 132, s. 4, prohibiting preferential assignments in contemplation of insolvency.—Brown v. Wilmington & Brandywine Leather Co., 74 A. 1105.

31-29. (Del. Ch.) Insolvency is sufficiently alleged in a bill which states that a corporation is unable to pay its debts as they mature, though other allegations should be included to invoke discretionary action.—Sill v. Kentucky Coal & Timber Development Co., 97 A. 617.

31-30. Where a stockholder in a domestic corporation sued to cancel stock unlawfully issued, and it was shown that there were deep-rooted dissensions between the stockholders of the corporation, that the business was unprofitable, and that complainant was the only stockholder who had invested money in the enterprise, a receiver pendente lite should be appointed, though none of the corporation's property was within the state, and though the receiver's power could not extend beyond the boundaries of the state; for, by General Corporation Law, s. 130, the capital stock of a domestic corporation is, for all purposes of title, action, attachment, etc., within the state, and, a receiver having been appointed within the state, ancillary receivership might be had in the states where the corporation's property was situated.—Ellis v. Penn Beef Co., 80 A. 666.

31d. Powers of Receiver.

31-31. (Del. Ch.) Receiver of corporation could proceed for unpaid subscriptions against administrator of party to whom original subscriber transferred stock to enable such party to qualify as director, though it was expressly agreed between original subscriber and transferee that latter should have no beneficial interest in shares.—Fell v. Securities Co. of North America, 100 A. 788.

31-32. (Del. Ch.) It is within inherent power of Court of Chancery to take possession of assets of corporation by a receiver pendente lite, in order to prevent loss.—Whitmer v. William Whitmer & Sons, 99 A. 428.

31-33. (Del. Ch.) A receiver for a corporation held not bound by its executory contracts.—Du Pont v. Standard Arms Co., 81 A. 1089, 9 Del. Ch. 315.

31-34. (Del. Ch.) A receiver of an insolvent corporation is an officer of the court, and takes only what the corporation had.—In re Frederica Water, Light & Power Co., 93 A. 376.

31-35. (Del. Ch.) An action against the officers and directors of a corporation for gross mismanagement must be brought by the receiver.—Du Pont v. Standard Arms Co., 82 A. 692, 9 Del. Ch. 324.

31-36. Where one of three liquidating trustees of a failing corporation acquired title to corporate property, the stockholders held entitled to avoid the transfer and participate in the profits on a resale.—Eberhardt v. Christiana Window Glass Co., 81 A. 774, 9 Del. Ch. 284.

31-37. Equity, in a suit by stockholders of a failing corporation will compel an accounting of profits by a liquidating trustee and a new corporation formed by him.—Eberhardt v. Christiana Window Glass Co., 81 A. 774, 9 Del. Ch. 284.

31-38. (Del. Ch.) Evidence held to show that directors of a failing corporation became liquidating trustees, with duties of such trustees.—Eberhardt v. Christiana Window Glass Co., 81 A. 774, 9 Del. Ch. 284.

See also Nos. 10-8, 14-46, 17-14.

31e. Claims Against Insolvent Corporations.

31-39. (Del. Ch.) Where insolvent corporation, as tenant, had agreed to pay 40 per cent. of cost of new building, and to pay 6 per cent. on balance of cost, and to purchase the building, and if the purchase was not made the new building to remain property of the landlord, a claim for the 60 per cent. will be disallowed in a receivership proceeding.—In re Receivership of Lightwell Steel Sash Co., 105 A. 376.

31-40. When there is insolvency and danger of losing money held by a corporation belonging to an individual, a creditor of the latter might, perhaps, go into equity and stop the money in the hands of the corporation.—S. C., 2 Harr. 306 (307).

31-41. (Del. Ch.) Fashion company's claim for liquidated damages against insolvent corporation for breach of contract to purchase patterns held provable.—In re Ross & Son, 95 A. 311.

31f. Rights of Creditors.

31-42. (Del. Ch.) Preference is given to the payment of rent in administering the estate of an insolvent corporation.—In re Receivership of Lightwell Steel Sash Co., 105 A. 376.

31-43. "Rent," entitled to preference in the administration of the estate of an insolvent corporation, is profit issuing out of land, and cannot reasonably include the cost of repairs which the tenant should have made, and which the landlord made, even if called rent.—In re Receivership of Lightwell Steel Sash Co., 105 A. 376.

31-44. Where insolvent corporation had, as a tenant, agreed to pay 40 per cent. of cost of a building to be erected, and 6 per cent. interest on the balance, and to buy the premises, the 40 per cent. to be allowed as a credit on the price, and if the purchase was not made the new building to remain the property of the landlord, the interest required to be paid was not rent, entitled to preferential payment, but can be allowed only as a general claim without priority.—In re Receivership of Lightwell Steel Sash Co., 105 A. 376.

31-45. (Del. Ch.) Despite General Corporation Law, s. 49, 51, creditor who had not secured judgment against corporation on which execution had been returned unsatisfied may, where receiver proceeds to enforce liability of holders for balance due on shares, have his claim satisfied out of such balance.—John W. Cooney Co. v. Arlington Hotel Co., 101 A. 879.

31-46. (Del. Ch.) Stockholders who took stock with notice of irregularities in issue thereof, and who extended credit to corporation, are not, because of their knowledge, estopped from participating as creditors after they have paid assessment levied for amounts due on their shares.—John W. Cooney Co. v. Arlington Hotel Co., 101 A. 879.

31-47. (Del. Ch.) A general manager of a corporation, discharged by a receiver, held not entitled to damages for termination of the contract.—Du Pont v. Standard Arms Co., 81 A. 1089, 9 Del. Ch. 315.

31-48. 17 Laws, c. 147, s. 7, 41, do not enable a creditor of an insolvent corporation to maintain an action on the case against a director for the amount of dividends withdrawn from the capital stock.—John A. Roebling's Sons Co., v. Mode (Del. Super.) 43 A. 480.

31-49. (Del. Ch.) The assets of an insolvent corporation are, in the absence of statute, administered according to equitable principles for the benefit of creditors generally, and the rule of marshaling assets does not apply, to the detriment of a single creditor holding security insufficient to pay his debts.—Mark v. American Brick Mfg. Co., 84 A. 887.

31-50. Independent of statute, a court of equity, administering the estate of an insolvent corporation, will allow a creditor holding collateral to prove and receive payment on his full claim, without deducting therefrom the amount obtained from the collateral, provided that in no event he receives more than his full debt from either or both sources.—Mark v. American Brick Mfg. Co., 84 A. 887.

31-51. A mortgagee of an insolvent corporation may share in the proceeds of its unmortgaged property administered in a court of equity, based on the full amount of the mortgage debt and interest thereon to the day of sale of the mortgaged property, provided he receives no more than the amount of his debt and interest.—Mark v. American Brick Mfg. Co., 84 A. 887.

31-52. A court of equity, administering the affairs of an insolvent corporation, may require a creditor, holding collateral, to realize on the collateral, or have it appraised, and the value, or the proceeds thereof, considered in the final settlement with him.—Mark v. American Brick Mfg. Co., 84 A. 887.

31-53. (Del. Ch.) Right to set off debts under Rev. Code 1852, amended to 1893, p. 793, c. 106, sec. 21, held not defeated by the appointment of a receiver for one of the parties, a corporation, on the ground of insolvency.—Grief v. James H. Wright Co., 91 A. 205.

31-54. A debt due to the receiver of an insolvent corporation, as distinguished from a debt due to the corporation, cannot be set off against a debt due from the corporation.—Grief v. James H. Wright Co., 91 A. 205.

31g. Stockholders' Liability for Unpaid Stock.

31-55. (Del.) In proceeding by receivers of an insolvent corporation to enforce stockholders' liability, it was inequitable to require the single stockholder found in the jurisdiction to pay the entire assessment, although such course was the most convenient for the receivers and expeditious for the creditors; but the receivers should have been ordered to collect every assessment they should find to be collectible, and that would justify the expense of collection, in order that the burden might be fairly distributed.—Du Pont v. Ball, 106 A. 39.)

31-56. (Del.) In proceeding by receivers of an insolvent corporation to enforce stockholders' liability for unpaid stock, the receivers are entitled to proper expenses and reasonable compensation to be paid by the stockholders.—Du Pont v. Ball, 106 A. 39.

31-57. (Del.) General Corporation Law (22 Del. Laws, c. 394, s. 20, providing that stockholders' liability for unpaid subscriptions may be enforced as provided for in section 49, which section provides for creditor's action at law, or bill in chancery, does not make such remedies exclusive, and such liability may be enforced by receivers in insolvency.—Du Pont v. Ball, 106 A. 39.

31-58. (Del.) The ordinary liability of a stockholder for unpaid subscription is an asset of the corporation, enforceable by its receivers upon insolvency, while a statutory liability for a sum in addition to unpaid subscriptions, as under a "double liability" statute, is not such an asset, but a liability directly to the creditors, which a receiver, in the absence of statutory authority, has no power to enforce.—Du Pont v. Ball, 106 A. 39.

31-59. Courts of domicile of corporation having appointed receiver on insolvency held that, where assessment against corporate stockholders for sums due on stock was necessary, such assessment may be made against resident stockholders who, on payment, can enforce contribution from others.—John W. Cooney Co. v. Arlington Hotel Co., 101 A. 879.

31-60. Where receivers of insolvent corporation petitioned that its debts be estimated and assessment levied against stockholders who had not fully paid for their shares, defense of limitations on ground of previous call for payment by corporate directors need not then be disposed of.—John W. Cooney Co., v. Arlington Hotel Co., 101 A. 879.

31-61. Corporate stockholders who had not fully paid for their shares cannot, where assessment is levied by court on petition of receivers, question propriety of assessment.—John W. Cooney Co. v. Arlington Hotel Co., 101 A. 879.

31-62. Where receivers in proceeding to assess stockholders who have not paid for their shares show that person is delinquent stockholder, etc., held, that assessment may be made on such prima facie case; receivers being allowed then by suit to test liability of such stockholder.—John W. Cooney Co. v. Arlington Hotel Co., 101 A. 879.

31-63. Certain defenses in proceeding by corporate receivers to levy assessment on holders of shares who had not paid therefor held personal to shareholder, and should not be adjudicated in assessment proceeding.—John W. Cooney Co. v. Arlington Hotel Co., 101 A. 879.

31-64. In proceeding by corporate receivers to levy assessment against shareholders who had not paid for their shares, held that defense that one was not shareholder would not be determined, but that he would be treated as such, appearing as shareholder on books. —John W. Cooney v. Arlington Hotel Co., 101 A. 879.

31-65. Where receivers of insolvent corporation petitioned for levy of assessment against shareholders who had not fully paid for their shares, those stockholders who had made payments on their stock in excess of their proportion of amount necessary to be levied should be excluded, and those stockholders who had made payments on account of their shares should be given credit therefor.— John W. Cooney Co. v. Arlington Hotel Co., 101 A. 879.

31-66. In case of insolvency of corporation, all moneys due from stockholders who have not paid for their stock constitute trust fund for creditors and there is no difference between preferred stockholders and common stockholders.—John W. Cooney Co. v. Arlington Hotel Co., 101 A. 879.

31-67. (Del.) In proceedings by receivers of insolvent corporation to assess stockholders on their liability for unpaid stock, interest on creditors' claims should commence at the time the receivers asked the court to make an assessment for the payment of such claims; there being nothing before which indicated that they would be expected to pay such claims.—Du Pont v. Ball, 106 A. 39.

31-68. (Del.) Where creditor proceeds in equity to secure the appointment of receivers on ground of insolvency of the corporation, obtaining a judgment and unsatisfied execution is not a condition precedent to enforcement by the receivers of stockholders' liability for unpaid subscriptions.—Du Pont v. Ball, 106 A. 39.

31-69. (Del. Ch.) Express assent of officers and directors of corporation to director's holding his qualifying shares of stock without beneficial interest as agent for another would not relieve director of liability on stock in favor of creditors of company.—Fell v. Securities Co. of North America, 100 A. 788.

See also No. 14-45.

31h. Distribution of Assets by Receiver.

31-70. (Del. Ch. 1910.) In distributing assets of an insolvent corporation among claimants, interest should be allowed only on claims of creditors who by their probated claims ask for interest, and those who do not will be assumed to have either waived it or not to be entitled to it.—Blair v. Clayton Enterprise Co., 77 A. 740.

31-71. Where funds are deposited in chancery by the receiver for distribution among creditors, he having been appointed under the act relating exclusively to insolvent corporations, they will be distributed to simple contract and judgment creditors alike.—In re Lord & Polk Chemical Co. (Del. Ch.) 44 A. 775.

31-72. In paying interest upon claims of creditors against an insolvent corporation, no difference should be observed between claims which bear interest according to the terms of the instrument upon which they are based and those which do not.—Blair v. Clayton Enterprise Co., 77 A. 740.

31-73. (Del. Ch. 1910.) Claims against an insolvent corporation, based upon notes, bonds, and book accounts, are on an equal footing; no one having priority of payment over the other.—Blair v. Clayton Enterprise Co., 77 A. 740.

32. RENEWAL OF CHARTERS
No decisions.

33. CORPORATE REORGANIZATIONS
No decisions.

34. FILING AND RECORDING FEES
No decisions.

35. FRANCHISE AND OTHER CORPORATE TAXES
No Decisions.

36. RECOGNITION AND MANNER OF QUALIFYING TO DO BUSINESS BY FOREIGN CORPORATIONS

36-1. (Del. Super. 1904.) That a corporation had filed a copy of its articles with the Secretary of State, and had appointed an authorized agent within the state, as required by Act March 23, 1903 (22 Del. Laws, p. 824, c. 395) did not make it a domestic corporation to such an extent as to relieve it from liability to be sued by process of foreign attachment.—Albright v. United Clay Production Co., 62 A. 726.

See also No. 28-9.

37. POWERS AND DUTIES OF FOREIGN CORPORATIONS

37a. Powers of Foreign Corporations.

37-1. (Del.) The right of a corporation to do business in a state or country other than that of its creation rests upon comity. (Super. 1910) Model Heating Co. v. Magarity, 75 A. 614, 1 Boyce, 240, judgment reversed (Sup. 1911) 81 A. 394.

37-2. (Del.) The question whether a contract made within the state by an agent of a foreign corporation can be enforced held properly raised by a plea in abatement.—Model Heating Co. v. Magarity, 81 A. 394, 2 Boyce, 459, L. .R A. 1915B, 665.

37-3. A foreign corporation, legally authorized and acting as administrator may, by its treasurer, make probate of a debt.—Derringer's Admr. v. Derringer's Admr., 6 Houst. 64 (79 et seq).

37-4. A corporation created and authorized by statute in another state to administer on the estates of deceased persons in that state, having done so, may sue as such administrator in the courts of this State for a debt due the decedent in this State.—Derringer's Admr. v. Derringer's Admr., 5 Houst. 416 (423).

37-5. The right of a corporation to carry on business in a foreign state, under its name, is not affected by the creation of a corporation in said state in the same name.—Reed v. Wilmington Steamboat Co. (Del. Super.) 40 A. 955.

37-6. A corporation can make contracts in other states, with such state's express or implied consent, and may be sued by service on its agencies in other jurisdictions.—Derringer's Admr. v. Derringer's Admr., 5 Houst. 416 (431).

See also Nos. 2-2, 6-12.

37b. Duties of Foreign Corporations.

37-7. A foreign corporation which is given certain rights by the laws of another state will be compelled to produce its books, in the hands of the president, residing in such other state, for inspection by a nonresident stockholder.—State v. Swift (Del. Super.) 30 A. 781.

37-8. Mandamus will not issue to compel a domestic corporation to aid a foreign corporation to conduct its business in Delaware.—State v. Delaware & A. Telegraph & Telephone Co. (Del. Super.) 31 A. 714.

See also Nos. 10-30.

38. DOING BUSINESS WITHOUT AUTHORITY

38-1. (Del.) A business which, by provision of Rev. Code 1852, amended to 1893, p. 56 (13 Del. Laws, c. 117), no one can engage in without first obtaining a license, cannot be conducted by a foreign corporation merely because of its doing the things required by the Constitution and statutes as a condition for a foreign corporation doing any business in the state.—E. A. Strout Co. v. Howell, 85 A. 666, 4 Boyce, 31.

38-2. (Del.) Under Const. 1897, art. 9, sec. 5, and Act March 23, 1903 (22 Del. Laws, c. 395), foreign corporation which has not complied with statutory provisions held entitled to enforce contract against purchaser, who retains benefits thereon.—Model Heating Co. v. Magarity, 81 A. 394, 2 Boyce, 459, L. R. A. 1915 B. 665.

38-3. (Del. Super.) A foreign corporation, not licensed as real estate broker, held not entitled to recover on a contract made with it as such.—E. A. Strout Co. v. Howell, 82 A. 238, 2 Boyce, 489.

38-4. (Del. Super. 1910.) Const. art. 9, s. 5, providing that no foreign corporation shall do business in the state through or by branch offices or agents located in the state, without having an authorized agent in the state upon whom legal process may be served, and 22 Del. Laws, c. 395, providing that it shall not be lawful for a foreign corporation to do business in the state through or by branch offices or agents until it shall have filed in the Secretary of State's office a certified copy of the charter, setting forth certain information, and the certificate of the Secretary of State shall be delivered to such agents, are a valid exercise of power in regulating foreign corporations.—Model Heating Co. v. Magarity, 75 A. 614, 1 Boyce, 240, judgment reversed (Sup. 1911) 81 A. 394.

38-5. (Del. Super. 1910). A foreign corporation having failed to comply with the statute, contracts executed by it are absolutely void, and it cannot recover thereunder.—Model Heating Co. v. Magarity, 75 A. 614, 1 Boyce 240, judgment reversed (Sup. 1911) 81 A. 394.

39. FEES, TAXES AND REPORTS OF FOREIGN CORPORATIONS

No decisions.

UNITED STATES CORPORATION COMPANY
AS AN AID
TO COUNSEL IN THE ORGANIZATION OF DELAWARE CORPORATIONS

Our company has a record of eighteen years of efficient service to the members of the bar. Its functions in assisting the lawyer in the organization of Delaware corporations are in part as follows:—

We verify the name of the proposed corporation.

We furnish official copies of the Corporation Law; a book of organization forms, carefully prepared for immediate use, and such other approved precedents and forms, as may be required.

On the instructions of counsel, we draft certificates of incorporation, by-laws and organization minutes for approval.

We attend to the filing and recording of certificates of incorporation, supplemental certificates and annual reports.

We furnish, if desired, incorporators who sign the certificate of incorporation, hold the incorporators' meeting, adopt by-laws, elect the first Board of Directors and immediately transfer to the parties in interest, their original subscriptions.

We furnish the principal office in the State of Delaware, display the sign required by statute, act as resident agent and keep the corporation in good standing in Delaware.

We notify the attorney of the time to file state reports, of the time to hold the annual meeting and of the time to pay the state taxes.

We also forward to the attorney all papers served upon the resident agent.

Upon the completion of the organization, we deliver to the attorney a complete minute book containing copies of the charter, by-laws and the organization minutes.

Other services rendered by the United States Corporation Company are as follows:

If the corporation is to transact business in other States and Countries, we draft the required qualification or registration papers upon the instructions of counsel. After approval and execution of the papers, we attend to the filing in the various states, securing licenses and permits, giving to counsel notices of State reports and taxes in the various jurisdictions.

We also furnish for a minimum fee the resident agent for service of process, when required, and forward all papers served upon the agent to the attorney.

For the convenience of members of the bar, we compile and distribute the Semi-Monthly Report Service which gives notice of every state report and tax required and of the similar reports and taxes in the Dominion and Provinces of Canada.

We also publish, for the convenience of counsel, the Corporation Manual, which contains in one volume, the corporation statutes of all of the States and Territories, the "Blue Sky" laws, the anti-trust laws and the uniform stock transfer act besides numerous forms and precedents.

In New York City, we maintain a large and active transfer department for the transfer and registration of corporate securities, and give an efficient and expeditious transfer service unequalled for its dispatch and accuracy.

EVERY CORPORATION SHOULD HAVE A TRANSFER AGENT

The function of a Transfer Agent is to

Keep the Records of the Stock Issued

to attend to the details of the

Issuance and Transfer of Stock

to see that all necessary transfer
tax stamps are affixed and cancelled, and to

Relieve the Officers of Routine and Responsibility

United States Corporation Company

ACTS as TRANSFER AGENT and REGISTRAR

at

65 CEDAR STREET, NEW YORK

United States Corporation Company

Executive Offices

65 CEDAR STREET

NEW YORK CITY

Howard K. Wood..............President

Dan Fellows Platt.............Treasurer

H. O. Coughlan ....Vice-President

L. H. Gunther ....Ass't. Treasurer

Arthur W. Britton ....Secretary

Geo. V. Reilly ....Ass't. Secretary

Samuel B. Howard ....Organization Secretary

James M. Satterfield...........................Dover Secretary

S. C. Wood............Chicago Secretary

L. K. Edmondson...,...St. Louis Secretary

S. V. Ryan...........,Albany Secretary

Wray C. Arnold.....Philadelphia Secretary

George V. Moore...........................Pittsburgh Secretary

---

⨌ Organizes and Maintains Foreign and Domestic Corporations in all States under supervision of counsel.

⨌ Acts as Transfer Agent and Registrar of Corporate Securities in New York City.

⨌ Publishes the Corporation Manual, containing the business corporation laws of all States under a uniform classification.

⨌ Issues the Semi-Monthly Report Service, which gives due dates of corporation reports and taxes.